When I Wear My
Alligator Boots

The publisher gratefully acknowledges the generous support of the Anne G. Lipow Endowment Fund for Social Justice and Human Rights of the University of California Press Foundation, which was established by Stephen M. Silberstein.

When I Wear My Alligator Boots

Narco-Culture in the U.S.-Mexico Borderlands

Shaylih Muehlmann

UNIVERSITY OF CALIFORNIA PRESS

Berkeley Los Angeles London

University of California Press, one of the most distinguished university presses in the United States, enriches lives around the world by advancing scholarship in the humanities, social sciences, and natural sciences. Its activities are supported by the UC Press Foundation and by philanthropic contributions from individuals and institutions. For more information, visit www.ucpress.edu.

University of California Press
Berkeley and Los Angeles, California

University of California Press, Ltd.
London, England

Library of Congress Cataloging-in-Publication Data

Muehlmann, Shaylih.
    When I wear my alligator boots : narco-culture in the
U.S.-Mexico borderlands / Shaylih Muehlmann.
        p.   cm.
    Includes bibliographical references and index.
    ISBN 978-0-520-27677-2 (cloth : alk. paper)
    ISBN 978-0-520-27678-9 (pbk. : alk. paper)
    1. Drug control—United States.   2. Drug control—
Mexican-American Border Region.   3. Drug traffic—
United States.   4. Drug traffic—Mexican-American
border Region.   5. Mexican-American Border Region—
Social conditions.   6. Rural poor—Mexico.   I. Title.
    HV5825.M77   2014
    363.450972'1—dc23   2013018892

Manufactured in the United States of America

23   22   21   20   19   18   17   16   15
10   9   8   7   6   5   4   3   2

Para Luz

CONTENTS

ILLUSTRATIONS

FIGURES

MAP

ACKNOWLEDGMENTS

My greatest debts acquired in the process of researching and writing this book are to those people who populate its pages and whose real names I cannot list here. For their kindness, hospitality, and generosity, I'd like to thank the men, women, and children in Mexico whose experiences brought this book to life. I'm also grateful to my wider network of support in Mexico, without whom this research would not have been possible and without whom writing this book would not have felt so important. To my *compadres*, godchildren, and friends and family in the desert north I give my sincere thanks.

I would also like to thank the members of the Caravana de la Paz, led by Javier Sicilia through the United States in 2012, for reminding me of the magnitude of this issue and for encouraging me to write for a larger audience. I'm particularly grateful to María Herrera Magdaleno, Rafael Trujillo Herrera, and Marco Antonio Castillo. I'm also thankful to Dean Becker and James E. Gierach for highlighting the ways the "war on drugs" has caused tremendous suffering in the United States as well as Mexico.

Writing this book involved some unpleasant periods of avoidance and reticence. There were a handful of people who helped me through some of these uncomfortable stages. I'm grateful to Max Ascrizzi, Terra Edwards, Andrea Kramer, Janet McLaughlin, Zoë H. Wool, and James Adam Redfield. I'd also like to thank Maya Jacob for talking me through more of this story than could ultimately be told in these pages.

This work has benefited immensely from the feedback and critical commentary offered by friends and family, as well as a number of my colleagues, both known and unknown. I'd like to thank my first readers, Scott Ryan Muehlmann, Patricia Ryan, Jimmy Ryan, and Robert Muehlmann, for important initial feedback. I'm very grateful to Alexander Dawson for his very insightful suggestions on the first draft of the manuscript and his continued advice and support. I'd also like to thank Adrienne Pine for her comments and encouragement. In addition, I'm grateful to the dozen or so anonymous reviewers who, on behalf of various granting agencies and journals, offered critical commentary on the manuscript at different stages. This feedback was crucial in honing my central argument and setting the tone for the book. I also appreciate the responses I received from members of the anthropology department at the University of Chicago at the beginning stages of conceptualizing this project. The research and editorial assistance provided by Danielle Good, Huma Mohibullah, Daniel Small, Taylor Davis Van Atta, and Clayton Whitt as well as the editorial support from the University of California Press were also very helpful at different stages of this project.

I wrote part of this book during a year as an Early Career Scholar at the Peter Wall Institute for Advanced Studies at the University of British Columbia. I'm grateful for the support I received from this institute as well as my cohort of interdisciplinary scholars, especially Amin Ghaziani, Kiley Hamlin, Janis Sara, and Andrew Martindale. There were several other institutions that supported the writing stage of this project financially. I'm grateful for the Hunt Scholarship from the Wenner-Gren Foundation for Anthropological Research and the Canada Research Chair program, both of which made possible precious time for writing.

I am, as usual, indebted to my core network of academic support: Jack Sidnell, Bonnie McElhinny, and William F. Hanks. I'd also like to thank my colleagues at the University of British Columbia, especially Julie Cruikshank, Bruce Miller, Patrick Moore, Carole Blackburn, Mike Richards, Juanita Sundberg, and Darlene Weston. Some of my more distant mentors and colleagues have been consistently supportive over the past few years and have thus eased the transitions involved in the search for employment and the subsequent trials of tenure tracking during which this book was written. I'd like to thank James F. Brooks, Jessica Cattelino, Benedict Columbi, Kristin Dowell, Les Field, and Anne Gorsuch for their various gestures of support.

Over the years of research and travel that went into this book I was blessed to have people who frequently provided me with shelter and company on my travels back and forth to the United States, Canada, and Mexico. I'm particularly grateful to Edward Blair, Virginia Buhr, Jake Flemming, Jana McQuilkin, Bridget Potter, Cory Silverberg, and Donna Sartonowitz for regularly taking me in when I passed through.

For advice, enlivenment, and encouragement, I'm grateful to Maureen Ryan, Joaquín Gordillo, Patrick Gabbert, Francis Beckett Van Atta, James Osip Van Atta, and Maressa Ryan. I would especially like to thank Robert Muehlmann and Patricia Ryan for not worrying too much but proofreading more than enough, as well as Rachel Ryan Muehlmann and Scott Ryan Muehlmann. With the utmost appreciation I also acknowledge Gastón Gordillo's talents as an ethnographer and a wordsmith and for being a superb accomplice in all things.

At last, a million thanks to the women in Mexico who have taken me in over the years and awed me with their resourcefulness, love, and humor. And for the guys at the fence, I offer my deep-felt gratitude for patiently explaining so much of what was already obvious to them, for inspiring me with their triumphs, as well as their losses, and foremost for volunteering themselves as my "new tribe."

Life at the Edges of the War on Drugs

When I first met Andrés he was working on a weed removal crew on a brackish tributary of the Colorado River in northern Mexico. It was a scorching August day: only 7 A.M. but already 100 degrees. Six of us were working by the side of the river cutting weeds in a work project for the local river users' association. The task was to take down the massive overgrowth of tamarisks, the invasive, water-sucking species that plagues the banks of the Colorado from Wyoming to Mexico. The crew was composed of young men from local communities. Andrés was there to make a living. I was there as a volunteer while doing research on the effects of water scarcity on local communities affected by the drying out of the once-lush Colorado Delta.

At 11 A.M., with a pounding headache from the sun, I retreated to the meager shade beside the association's truck for a break. I could only do this because I was a volunteer. The rest would get 100 pesos (about US$10) for eight hours of work. So they continued their work for another three hours in the blazing sun, ripping out roots with their hands, thrashing the dense thicket with machetes hauling the refuse into piles, and finally setting it all on fire.

During one break, the others joined me to crouch in the shade and drink water under the smoke from the fire. We were all clothed from head to toe to protect us from the sun's rays and soaked with sweat. Andrés wore an oversized long-sleeved shirt and faded blue jeans tucked into a pair of muddy rubber boots. I asked him how he usually made his living, since the tamarisk cut was just a few days of work. He spoke softly from under the brim of his wide wicker hat. He described how he worked odd jobs such as this one when they presented themselves; sometimes he worked building roads through the desert, extracting gravel, or piling stones and sometimes as a helper on fishing crews. For a while, the conversation turned to rumors of the huge wages that one can make in the United States. One man asked me if it was true that over there you could make up to $14 an hour in a job like this. The minimum wage in northern Mexico at the time was 40 pesos a day (about US$4), so the tamarisk cut was not a bad day's work, they agreed. But Andrés commented that he thought Mexican wages were not fair since it is very hard to find enough work to cover even the basic cost of living.

Several months later, I saw Andrés again. He pulled up in a new pickup beside the house where I was staying. Along with my companions Javier and Isabella, I watched as he stepped out of the truck in beige alligator boots, a wide belt with a metal buckle, and a cowboy hat. He looked so different that at first I wasn't sure if he was the same guy. "Who is that?" I asked, startled. "That's Andrés," Javier said. I was still confused. "That's the same Andrés from Santa Ana who worked for the tamarisk project?" I pressed, still not quite believing it was the same person. "Yeah, it's Andrés. I bet you think he's handsome," Javier said, in an accusing tone. Isabella jumped in to affirm, "He looks sooo handsome." I ignored her and explained, "He just looks really different from the last time I saw him." Javier nodded knowingly, "Yeah, he's going around all *cholo* [like a gang member] now, isn't he?" Isabella let out a drawn-out sigh, and Javier frowned, watching Andrés with a mixture of envy and disdain.

Andrés, it soon became clear, had come to sell drugs to one of our neighbors. I was not surprised to learn of Andrés's career change from working poorly paid odd jobs to selling drugs and, as I learned later, smuggling. I had seen enough people move in and out of trafficking or smuggling and also the relentless lack of other forms of viable work. But I was surprised to see how visible Andrés's transformation was. He was dressed in the restrained version of the classic *chero* (cowboy) style associated in the region at that time with *narcos* or *narcotraficantes,* "narcotraffickers." The alligator boots were the signature touch, as Javier had mentioned several times before: "It's how you tell a *real* narcotraficante."

ON NOT ASKING QUESTIONS ABOUT THE WAR ON DRUGS

I first visited Mexico looking for potential field sites for my doctoral research in 2003, and then I moved to northern Mexico in 2005 to spend a year doing fieldwork. My plan was to head right past the tumult of drug activity and violence that I had read about in the border cities. I was going to the desert south of the U.S.-Mexico border where I thought I would be far away from the violence of cartel politics and fully ensconced in the everyday routines of the rural communities that were struggling to navigate extreme environmental degradation.

In fact, I had every intention of avoiding the topic of the "drug wars" altogether. Since 2000, sixty-eight reporters have been shot down in Mexico for reporting on drug-related activity and government corruption, forty-seven of them slain between July 2008 and September 2010.[1] Not one of those murders has been solved. It was clear that the drug trade was a topic that was dangerous to explore, but in thinking I could avoid the subject, I was profoundly underestimating how deeply the narco-economy affects people's lives. In the end, it was not up to me whether to pursue the topic: people came to me with their stories.

In the first few months of my fieldwork, while I was still largely unaware of the extent to which the narco-world pervaded the local economy, I was nonetheless struck by the fact that the drug trade was a persistent feature of gossip and everyday conversation. For example, every few days I would sit for several hours with Esperanza, a seventy-four-year-old woman who had lived in the area all her life. We would talk, and I would record her experiences about growing up in the region. She would interrupt her own stories to comment on every vehicle or body that passed. She saw Andrés making his rounds in his new truck, and she watched his every move. "Look who just stopped in there with Daniela," she'd say. "They are going to buy drugs, you know. *Pura drogas, puro drogadictos, andando cristalino.* All drugs, all drug addicts, going around high on crystal."

While Esperanza's imputations of narco-involvement were especially dramatic (she claimed that most of her neighbors were, if not addicts, full-fledged *mafiosos*), her attitude was characteristic of the way locals often talked about their neighbors. At first, I tried to ignore this kind of talk. To me, Esperanza's accusations represented an internalization of a common stereotype of Mexico's rural poor. But as in many of the poor villages located in the cartel territories of the border, local involvement with the drug trade is much more mundane than Esperanza imagined. Those who are directly involved fill the most vulnerable and exploited roles in the economy—drug addiction, petty sales, stashing, and smuggling—rather than roles in the high-profile network of killers and cutthroat businessmen who run the cartels. Nonetheless, Esperanza's insistence on the topic was important because it emphasized that the narco-economy's effect on this community was central to the experience of those who lived there.

The traces of the drug trade are, in fact, everywhere in the U.S.-Mexico borderlands: from the gang violence in the border cities and drug addiction in rural enclaves to the vibrant folklore popularized in the Norteña *narco-corridos* (ballads lionizing narcos) and the icons of Jesús Malverde (the patron saint of narcos) tucked beneath the shirts of local people. Prohibition efforts also trod heavily over the landscape, from the subtler traces such as the diagonal ditches gouged out of the desert to prevent clandestine plane landings to the ominous presence of military lookouts and checkpoints that have visibly transformed the region into an occupied territory (figure 1).

While the specter of drug-related violence in Mexico has had a powerful media presence in the past few years, the story of those who are most vulnerable to the dangers of drug trafficking, and most susceptible to the promise of its rewards, is seldom told. This book tells the story of rural people living in the U.S.-Mexico borderlands who are recruited to work in the lowest echelons of the drug trade, as *burreros* (mules) and low-level narcotraficantes. These people do not live in the epicenters of drug-associated violence, such as the urban battlegrounds of Juárez

Figure 1. Notches cut in the desert to prevent clandestine landings.
Photo by author.

and Tijuana, but in the far rural outskirts of such border cities. They live at the edges of the "war on drugs," where both the trade and violence and the hope it generates nonetheless permeate everyday life.

Rather than chronicle the lives of the high-profile cartel leaders, my focus is on ordinary people working and living at the fringes of the narco-economy. This is not the story of the powerful capos but of the women who make them their sandwiches, the businessmen who launder their money, the addicts who consume their product, the mules who carry their money and drugs through borders and military checkpoints, and the men and women who serve out the prison sentences when the capos' operations go awry.

This book shows that the drug trade functions not just through the acts of the violent, murderous figures represented in the media, but crucially through networks of ordinary people and legitimate businesses, in ways that profoundly imbricate everyday life. Through the stories of individual people who have become involved in the drug trade in various ways this book seeks to complicate the very notion that there is a definable "in" and "out" of the trade. I argue that this distinction dissolves, not just for the rural poor in northern Mexico, but also for the wealthy nations and institutions that have both profited from the war on drugs and imposed the policies that underwrite the tremendous bloodshed and suffering this war has unleashed.

ALONE, IN THE MIDDLE OF THE DESERT, WITH A BUNCH OF NARCOS

It was late one night in Santa Ana, and I was sitting against a fence with three young men. One of them, Álvaro, was the most active in local smuggling and trafficking among the people I knew in the area. We were all drinking beer, and the men were casually boasting about their experiences transporting drugs across the border. We were slightly tipsy and laughing a lot. Their stories were full of funny anecdotes about evading the cops and cheating their bosses. Spirits were high. And so it caught me off guard when Álvaro turned directly to me and said, "Hey, how come you're not scared to be hanging out with us?"

"What?" I said, startled. "What do you mean?" Álvaro was quick to jump in with a rather convincing rationale. "Well, you're a white girl from Canada hanging out in the middle of nowhere, in the middle of the desert, with a bunch of narcos." I laughed nervously but was quick to respond in my own defense. "Well you're not *just* a bunch of narcos," I said, maybe a bit too hopefully. "I've known you all for a while. Besides, I totally trust these guys." I motioned over to Andrés, who at the time of this conversation I knew a lot better than Álvaro. I noticed how young he looked, grinning up at Álvaro with an expression of reverence and subservience. "And I know Javier always has my back," I continued. I had been living with Javier's family for almost a year. But as I motioned over to him I couldn't help but notice that he was a lot drunker than I had realized. He was slumped against the fence with his white baseball cap turned backwards. I scrambled for the pack of cigarettes that had been dangling farther and farther out of Javier's breast pocket. "Besides, you're not so bad, Álvaro," I said, lighting a cigarette in a self-conscious display of nonchalance, "despite your reputation ..."

Álvaro laughed and launched into a long, complicated story about what an upstanding guy he is, despite all the trouble he gets into. Fortunately, my reaction seemed to have appeased him. I had acknowledged his badass reputation but also implied that I trusted him anyway. The truth is that I was not sure whether Álvaro was offended because I wasn't more scared of him, whether he was giving me credit for being brave, or whether he was pointing out how naive I'd been to have gotten myself into this situation in the first place. While they resumed the lively conversation, I was left ruminating on the self-evident truth of that third interpretation. I was, indeed, alone in a dusty little village in the middle of the desert hanging out with a bunch of narcos.

I had ended up in this situation through the kind of contingencies that are common in anthropological fieldwork. I had originally found a place to live in a small mestizo fishing village not far from Santa Ana with Javier's family. I was introduced to Ana, Javier's mother, at a birthday party for a little girl who was turning four. Ana and I became friendly quite quickly, and not long after she invited me to stay with her family. Ana lived with her husband, Cruz, son, Javier, and eighteen-year-old twin daughters, Ruby and Berenice. Ana's family was the first of several that over the past ten years have generously invited me into their homes to stay for stretches of fieldwork. My stay with Ana's family was foundational, however, because in their home I learned to speak Spanish and established a network of friends and contacts throughout the fishing villages of the region. It was also in their home that I became familiar with some of the basic conditions of life of rural people in northern Mexico.

During the first few weeks in Ana's family home, I came to realize that it was not only the impact of narcotrafficking that was being felt by local communities but also drug addiction. Cruz, it turned out, was addicted to crystal meth. But it took me a while to put this together. At first, I noticed that he would often stay up all night, and I was confused by his nocturnal activities: he would pace around the back of the house sweeping and fiddling with the empty shell of a truck. Sometimes I would hear him sweeping the sandy earth for hours out in front of the house. This was especially puzzling to me. Why was it important to keep the sand smooth? Because I had just started my research on themes quite unrelated to drugs, my initial response was to find some "cultural" explanation for the insistence on order and smoothness in front of the house. Cruz's fixation contrasted dramatically with the mayhem inside the home. Why didn't he obsess over the flies, garbage, and dust inside?

The drug that Cruz was addicted to, methamphetamine, is a psycho-stimulant popularly known as crystal meth and *cristal* or *foco* in Spanish. Cristal acts as a powerful and immediate stimulant to the central nervous system, causing sensations of euphoria and excitement. As I later learned, users often become fixated on performing repetitive tasks such as cleaning, hand-washing, and assembling and disassembling objects. Hence Cruz's enthusiastic sweeping.[2]

While the wreckage of drug addiction in rural villages of the area was my introduction to the way the narco-region was taking its toll on its residents, drug addiction and use is not the primary focus of this book (though I explore the topic in chapter 4). I am more concerned about telling a story of how the narco-economy itself has emerged as an economic alternative to fishing, factory work, and other income-earning strategies available in the local legal economy. I examine the rise of narcotrafficking and smuggling as one of the economic alternatives sought by local people, and I explore how the economy of the drug trade has emerged concomitantly with powerful cultural and affective forms and associations that I trace to a legacy of border violence and a history of antagonistic relations between the United States and Mexico.

PROHIBITION, NAFTA, AND THE WAR ON DRUGS

I ended up in the middle of a major drug trafficking corridor through the contingencies of fieldwork. Locals, however, ended up in the midst of the war on drugs by way of a longer trajectory of historical and political contingencies. Until the 1980s drug smuggling in Mexico had remained a regionally based activity, because Colombian groups dominated international trade. The U.S. crackdown on Colombian drug trafficking organizations in the 1980s disrupted not only the traditional routes for cocaine smuggling, through the Caribbean and South Florida, but also the preferred method of smuggling, which was by aircraft (Andreas 2009: 52). The impact of the intensified U.S. pressure on smuggling patterns was to shift the flow of drugs to the southwestern border of the United States and redirect, rather than reduce, smuggling, by pushing trade out of the air and into the road transportation networks connecting Mexico with the United States. The U.S. Drug Enforcement Agency (DEA) estimates that now 90 percent of all narcotics smuggled into the United States enter from Mexico.[3]

Drug cartels in Mexico expanded significantly in the twenty years following the collapse of the major Colombian organizations (Campbell 2009). This process was facilitated in part by Mexico's signing of the North American Free Trade Agreement (NAFTA) in 1994. The flooding of Mexico with cheap agribusiness-produced corn put many Mexican farmers and rural workers out of business, and many turned to drug cultivation and trade as an alternative. Increased legal trade between the United States and Mexico also facilitated increased illegal trade, because the same routes could be used to smuggle narcotics across the border with much more ease. Therefore, NAFTA played a major role in the rise of narcotrafficking cartels in Mexico (Andreas 1995, 2009; Malkin 2001).

Although the fact that the drug trade and neoliberal economic policies actually reinforce each other is rarely admitted openly in U.S. public policy debates, the very logic of neoliberalism is for the state to give way to international market pressures.[4] Andreas points out that the market does not recognize state-created distinctions between the legal and illegal spheres and that the illicit drug industry is a leading market force and an integral component of the private sector. Therefore, neoliberalism has a symbiotic relationship with the very illegal market that the United States claims to prohibit (Andreas 1995: 76).

A truck driver I met, who people called El Chibo, "the Goat," was the first to spark my interest in how NAFTA has stimulated the drug economy. The trucking industry is a concrete illustration of this trend: when borders opened up for trade in the 1990s the volume of trucks crossing the border increased dramatically. The number of trucks crossing has tripled since the signing of NAFTA, and there is no way that more than a fraction of them can go through inspections without affecting the legal flow of goods as well.[5]

I met El Chibo, who was in his late thirties at the time, when he was dating my friend Isabella. He would take shipments packed into compartments on the underside of his trailer, whose top was full of the fruits and vegetables or whatever kind of legal shipment he would also be responsible for. He said that he was paid a lot of money to cross the border depending on how much he took. Traffickers could pack several hundred pounds of cocaine into the compartments of his eighteen-wheeler.

El Chibo explained that this was a fairly common mode of transporting drugs. People build special compartments into their cars so that they can pack in shipments, and it is one of the easiest ways to make cash if you can make it across. When I asked if he started off as a smuggler or a trucker, he said that he was just a trucker first. About six years earlier, he started to hear of more and more truck drivers working as "blind mules." Smugglers hide drugs in the vehicles of people who regularly cross the border without their being aware of it, follow the cars, and then retrieve the loads on the other side.[6]

El Chibo said that some of his coworkers went to jail for taking a load they didn't even know they had until they were caught. So truckers started watching their rigs 24/7, never leaving them for an instant. He said it got to the point where he was so paranoid about his rig and so nervous going through the border crossing that he decided he might as well sign on and get paid to haul the loads. "I figured it was better than unknowingly taking a load and not getting paid," he said. Once he made up his mind it was easy to find a connection with a supplier, for truck drivers are consistently propositioned to haul drugs (this is also the case for commuters). In fact, Andreas (1996: 58) explains that the use of trucking as a mode of smuggling became so common after NAFTA that traffickers actually hired consultants to determine what kinds of products get through faster than others, such as perishable or electronic goods.[7]

The extent to which organized illegal syndicates have infiltrated Mexican export and trucking companies is well known to U.S. federal law enforcement and Mexican security sources.[8] As trade was stimulated by liberalizing economic agreements and the expansion of the trucking industry, however, mounting prohibition efforts continued to attempt to selectively thwart the flow of illicit goods. The escalating tensions created by these contradictory efforts resulted in an even more violent upsurge in 2006 with the militarization of the war on drugs.

In December 2006, shortly after taking office, former president Felipe Calderón launched a military offensive against the drug cartels. The violence associated with the drug trade and its impact on society have escalated significantly since then. Official government discourses and the mainstream media explain the horrific violence since 2006 as resulting from rivalries among cartels and have portrayed the militarization as an effort to "suppress" this bloodshed.

Instead, many observers have argued, the violence has skyrocketed because of the militarization of the war on drugs.[9] Since 2006, seventy thousand people have been killed nationwide. Domestic and international human rights organizations have documented record-breaking numbers of human and civil rights violations on the part of Mexican federal forces. While three in four Mexicans say cartel-related violence is a very big problem for the country, roughly an equal number say the same about human rights violations by the military and police.[10] The murders continue not only despite the presence of thousands of soldiers and federal agents on the streets, but partly because of it, which has led many people to question the government's strategy.[11]

This ongoing devastation is partially produced and sustained by the illegality of drugs. It is because drugs are illegal commodities that manufacturing them and distributing them is so extraordinarily lucrative. That the United States and Mexico continue to impose a "war" that has been such a spectacular failure is also enormously lucrative for both the countries and the markets involved. As astounding as the profits of the drug trade are to the cartels, the overwhelming majority of the profits made from drug production and trafficking go to the wealthy consuming countries, primarily the United States, rather than producing nations such as Mexico.[12] The drug trade has also underwritten enormous profits for the weapons manufacturing industries and big-budget federal agencies such as the DEA and the Department of Homeland Security. Prohibition policies and U.S. and Mexican interdiction efforts have not stopped the flow of drugs but instead, I suggest, have outsourced to Mexico much of the violence associated with the trade.

There have long been leading commentators and economists across the political spectrum who have challenged the logic of prohibition policies. More recently, heads of state and government across Latin America as well as scholars and policy makers have increasingly argued that the only way to bring an end to narco-associated violence is the decriminalization of the drug trade, primarily in the United States. They argue that by legalizing and regulating use, prices would drop, the illicit trade would collapse, and Mexican cartels would lose their portion of the global drug profit, which the UN Office on Drugs and Crime (UNODC) has estimated amounts to $320 billion per year.[13]

While the focus of this book is not the issue of legalization, the experiences I describe have a bearing on discussions of drug prohibition policies. Arguments for legalization are certainly no longer novel or marginal.[14] The economic and political arguments for decriminalization, however, have failed to sway the opinions of the majority of the American public. I hope that the ethnographic perspective of this book will bring to life what's at stake in the policy debate by illustrating the impacts of criminalization on people's lives.

There are a number of deeply naturalized assumptions about the drug trade that allow prohibition policies to make sense to people in the United States and Mexico. One is that by prohibiting drugs they will be less accessible, thereby decreasing addiction rates and reducing their harmful effects. This assumption has repeatedly been shown to be untrue. Across the United States, and now Mexico, addiction rates and availability have increased with prohibition.[15] The local dynamics of this effect of prohibition policies are discussed in chapter 4.

Another assumption that undergirds public support for prohibition is more central to the argument of this book. This is the idea that drug trafficking organizations are set apart from society in cartels or gangs that are composed of brutal criminals working outside the law. This assumption has been complicated in recent years as the degree of collusion between the military, police, and organized crime has been increasingly well documented in Mexico. By now it is well known that authorities are often paid off by narcos to gain access to guarded trade routes and that certain cartels have long-term arrangements providing privileged access to checkpoints, crossings, money laundering operations, and political decision making.[16]

But there are other kinds of alliances, more visible in the everyday workings at the edges of the drug trade, that further complicate the distinctions between "legal" and "illegal" actors and shape the networks in which drugs are produced and distributed. A man named José told me the story of his first experience in short-distance smuggling, which illustrates such alliances. José had agreed to do a pickup of an incoming shipment. He was supposed to meet a plane in the desert, help unload the shipment, and then transport it to a nearby contact who would arrange for the rest of the load's journey. José did as he was told, and the operation went smoothly until he started driving away with the load and the plane took off. At that moment a truck full of soldiers appeared and approached his vehicle. José was petrified, but as the truck neared, he recognized one of the soldiers, Antonio, who was the husband of his niece Lupita. As the soldiers searched the vehicle and discovered the drugs, José and Antonio had an awkward encounter. In the end, Antonio convinced the soldiers to let his uncle José go.

I never became close enough with Antonio, the soldier, to ask him directly about how family obligations affected his work generally. But Lupita told me that encounters such as these were one of the reasons that her husband preferred not to be stationed in the area. He had done well for himself in the military, escaping the poverty of his upbringing, and had even won a medal from the government for his work intercepting smugglers. But he was not able or willing to extract himself from the web of relationships, both his own family's and Lupita's, in which he was embedded and that permeated the region. He felt compromised by encounters such as the one with José and the shipment of drugs. Not long after that incident he put in a request to be transferred to a station outside of Mexico City.

José and Antonio's encounter in the desert is just one of many that illustrate the difficulty of determining the boundaries of organized crime in a region that has been so thoroughly engulfed by a powerful economy fueled by the demand for drugs in the United States, as well as a political and legal framework that has been compromised by the incentives of meeting this demand. Most important, José and Antonio's encounter in the desert highlights the fact that when individuals align themselves with and against "legal" or "illegal" bodies, they do so in the context of their own lives and relationships, as well as the debts and obligations they owe their families.

This book shows that the drug trade does not exist separately from society. It functions through networks of ordinary people attempting to survive in the starkly unequal social and economic conditions of the U.S.-Mexico borderlands.

THE NARCO-ALLURE IN THE U.S.-MEXICO BORDERLANDS

The village of Santa Ana is one of many rural settlements that happen to be located in geographic coincidence with the narco routes stretching across the desert corridor between San Felipe, Mexicali, and Tijuana: the principal throughway for drugs from the Gulf of California (see map 1). This is a region characterized by a harsh desert climate, with extremes that alternate between daytime temperatures of up to 110 degrees Fahrenheit and nighttime temperatures that sometimes plummet to 32 degrees Fahrenheit. The area is also bisected by the San Andreas Fault, which runs a length of roughly 810 miles (1,300 km) through California to Mexico. The fault forms the tectonic boundary between the Pacific Plate and the North American Plate, and these shifting plates mean that one is more likely to experience an earthquake in this region than a rainfall.

In many rural villages smuggling pays relatively good wages and provides better working conditions, in general, than the *maquiladora* (assembly plant) industry or the informal day labor that has come to characterize the "legal" face of economic development in the region. For these reasons, the narco-economy

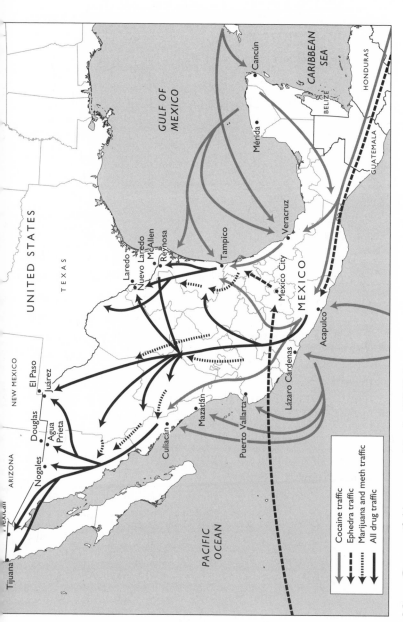

Map 1. Drug trafficking routes. Map by Bill Nelson.

presents an alternative to social and economic marginalization. For instance, Álvaro, who was thirty-three when I first met him, explained that he began trafficking the year that officials confiscated the equivalent of US$1,000 worth of his fishing nets in the Gulf of California due to his purported violation of environmental restrictions. Álvaro had been fishing since the age of six and could not imagine how he was going to survive without his nets. He recounted what he said to the officials that day on the water: "Who is going to support my family if you take away my nets? Are *you* going to support my family?" In Álvaro's understanding, his turn to narcotrafficking was a response to being denied the right to work by the Mexican government.

While many people talked about the draw of the trade in the logic of financial incentive, what became increasingly clear over the course of my fieldwork was that there was a less obvious allure that was equally significant. As I discuss in chapters 2 and 3, the drug trade allows some people, especially young men, to draw on the sense of pride and defiance that characterizes the popular northern Mexican persona of the narcotraficante and the rich cultural matrix from which this figure emerges. The persona of the traficante resonates historically with a legacy of U.S.-Mexican antagonism on the border that has been fueled by the militarization of the region and the lack of other viable routes of upward mobility.

In many ways, the drug trade and the cultural forms that have emerged in tandem with it have led to a celebration of drug trafficking and sometimes its violence. This is most noticeable among the region's youth. In the first year that I lived in the area, I became friends with a young boy named Samuel. At fifteen, he had been mixed up in mundane, relatively harmless ways with the drug trade. He was involved with drug traffickers in the way that many local kids in this region of poor fishing villages were. They would run down to the boat landings and unload shipments. They would often do this with their parents' blessing and would get paid on the spot for their manual labor. Others were recruited as lookouts to spot the police or the military. This was not a secret among locals, and some of the kids boasted about it. For them, this was an exciting activity, a brush with a powerful underworld that is celebrated in popular culture.

One day Samuel told me, in confidence, that a few times "they" asked him to do more dangerous things. He said, in a boasting tone, that they had paid him to shoot two people on two separate occasions. I was shocked by Samuel's confession. Despite the incongruity between the image I had of him and the idea that he was an assassin, I believed him at that time. He sounded sincere, scared, and remorseful. By then it had become fairly common to hear of the cartels recruiting very young children, between the ages of ten and fifteen, to work as hit men, for as juveniles they receive lesser sentences if caught.

After a few more years of going back to the area, I've come to suspect that Samuel's confession was nothing more than a childish boast meant to sound impressive. I've watched Samuel as he has grown up over nearly a decade and now works for his mother-in-law's fishing crew. His wife is pregnant with their second child. Kids who work as hit men at such a young age don't usually make their way out of the trade. Santa Ana is also an out-of-the-way place; cartels and gangs tend to pick up child assassins in urban neighborhoods such as those in Juárez or Tijuana.

Samuel's boasting that he was a child assassin was disturbing in ways that went beyond the truth or falsity of his claim. It reveals that in parts of northern Mexico you can impress some people by saying that you have killed. Under what kinds of violent conditions could such a positive association with murder be generated among working-class youth? This is one of the questions this book explores.

RESEARCHING THE EFFECTS OF
THE WAR ON DRUGS

Because the drug trade was such a powerful part of the way locals were experiencing the changing economic conditions of the border, I began actively collecting stories and experiences about the narco-economy and its effects on people in the region in 2005 and continued my research for this book up to my last trip to the area in 2013. In addition, in August 2012 I joined a caravan of victims of the drug war—men and women who had lost loved ones to the violence—as they traveled through parts of the United States protesting U.S. and Mexican drug war policies. The people I met on this trip helped broaden and inform aspects of this book and place my prior ethnographic research in a more national and binational context.

Much of what I originally learned about the effect of the drug trade and the war on drugs on local communities was through a general interest in the everyday conditions of life in the region. I did not decide to write a book specifically on the topic until 2009, years after I started doing ethnographic research there. Therefore, a large part of what I document in this book I learned without having a clear scholarly agenda but rather from a general research interest in the region as well as a personal interest in the people I had become close to as a result of doing fieldwork in local communities over several years.

My principal method for gathering ethnographic material was participant observation: by spending long stretches of time with people and interacting with them in everyday activities. Through semistructured interviews, I also gathered accounts of local experiences of the rise of the narco-economy. I recorded life histories of individuals whose stories were emblematic of certain facets of the drug trade's local impact. But most of these interviews have ultimately been put to use here in fleshing out the stories of a handful of key individuals whom I came to know well and was able to interact with over a span of several years.[17]

The difficulty of highlighting individuals in ethnographic accounts is that they may be taken as "typical" and their experiences generalizable well beyond their personal trajectories. I want to avoid portraying the people I've come to know as representative types: Paz is not a typical "narco-mom" any more than Andrés is a typical narco or Cruz a classic meth-head. Instead, I hope that by carefully detailing the lives of sometimes quite exceptional people, I will be able to reveal the nature of processes that are characteristic of everyday experiences in the region. While I focus on the life trajectories of a handful of key people, my analysis does not rely on these individuals' narrations alone. In addition to analyzing these individuals' own accounts of their life histories, and my interviews with them, I attend to ethnographic evidence I gathered during long-term participant observation of their lives and practices.[18]

The book begins with the stories of Andrés's mother, Doña Paz, and his girlfriend, Isabella, as they waited out his prison sentence, and of Andrés as he adjusted to life after prison. Then I explore my friend Cruz's addiction to cristal and how the prohibition on drugs has shaped his family and his experience of dependence. I analyze the experiences of several mules smuggling drugs and money through military checkpoints. Along the way, we meet meth orphans, truck drivers, former priests, corrido fans, money launderers, and aspiring narco-wives.

Writing about drug abuse and illegal activities presents potential risks for those whose lives are being chronicled. Throughout the book, I use pseudonyms for both names and places in order to maintain people's anonymity. Following in the direction of other authors who have written about individuals involved in the drug trade, I also take additional care to obscure identities by modifying details of individuals' biographies and at points merging or separating details to further complicate possible attempts to identify individuals.[19] I use the fictitious place-name "Santa Ana" to stand in for the several villages in which I did research and to localize the narrative of the book.

Through the stories of Álvaro, Cruz, and others, the chapters that follow reveal a tension at the heart of the so-called war on drugs. For many men and women living in poverty, the narco-economy represents an alternative to the exploitation and alienation they experience trying to work in the borderland's legal economy, increasingly dominated by the presence of U.S.-owned maquiladoras and ravaged by environmental degradation. Despite the lawlessness and violence brought on by the war on drugs and the ruinous consequences this has had for some of the most vulnerable people involved, narcotrafficking and smuggling represent one of the few promises of upward mobility for the poor in Mexico's north. It is not simply economic conditions that have facilitated the induction of low-level workers into the drug trade, however, but also a larger cultural context and a legacy of violence in which the persona of the narcotraficante plays a crucial role.

Media representations of drug violence in Mexico, which focus on the men who do the killing and are predominantly those who are killed, make women's roles in the trade as well as their suffering invisible. In chapter 1, I follow the stories of several women whose experiences were revealing about the nature of the narco presence in the region and especially the way this presence is felt by women. These are the other faces of the drug wars: mothers, wives, and daughters waiting for their sons, husbands, and fathers to serve out their prison sentences or mourning their deaths and disappearances.

Chapter 2 examines how the narco-economy allows people to retain a sense of pride and defiance drawn from the popular northern Mexican persona of the narcotraficante. In particular, it follows Andrés's experience adjusting to life as a former narcotraficante. When Andrés got out of jail, he vowed he would not get involved with the mafia again, but in the months that followed, he struggled with his loss of prestige. This chapter explores the larger cultural context through which the local glorification and social prestige of the narcotraficante is more easily understood.

Chapter 3 delves deeper into the cultural context and impact of the drug trade by analyzing how narco-corridos, a genre of folk song, have become extremely popular in northern Mexico over the past few decades. Corridos are ballads that tell the history of men and women working in the drug business, venerating the lives of famous narcotraffickers and often commissioned by the traffickers themselves. Efforts to ban and censor the songs have become more forceful in the past few years, as government officials have argued that the songs are part of the cause of the narco-related violence. I show, in contrast, that corridos are coproductive of an affective and embodied sensibility that doesn't just celebrate violence but also challenges silencing and censorship.

While the consumption of drugs in the United States, rather than Mexico, tends to be emphasized in policy discussions and media accounts, in chapter 4 I show how an important impact of the narco-trade in the everyday lives of people in the borderlands is drug addiction. The U.S. prohibition has increased the circulation of drugs through northern Mexico, and as a result, some drugs have become widely accessible and relatively affordable. In this chapter, I examine drug addiction as one of the important material effects of both poverty and prohibition on the rural poor in Mexico's north.

Because the United States is by far the largest consumer of drugs in the world, the estimated $20 billion to $30 billion of drug money that flows into the Mexican economy each year, for the most part, starts its path in the United States.[20] It comes back to drug cartels in Mexico through a variety of illicit routes and often on the bodies of smugglers. In chapter 5, I analyze the experiences of burreros in northern Mexico who smuggle thousands of American dollars in cash, hidden on their bodies, through military checkpoints. This chapter engages dominant narratives about modern finance that emphasize that we live in a time of economic virtualism when financial activities have increasingly moved toward abstraction. I show how this narrative of abstraction could not be more distant from the experience of smugglers in Mexico.

In chapter 6, I analyze one of the key organizing features of how people understand their own position in relation to the drug trade: the concept of risk and the kinds of moral and economic calculations that are figured into the decisions people make about their involvement in the trade. I argue that many get involved in the drug trade because it seems riskier for them *not* to get involved, as the example of the truck driver presented earlier illustrates.

The people whose lives are chronicled in this book reveal the extent to which the war on drugs ultimately pushes many of the costs of trafficking—the deaths, the vulnerability, and the risk—over the border into Mexico and particularly onto the Mexican poor. These are the people who run the risks of the business, experience the brunt of the violence, and serve the prison sentences that the wealthy cartel bosses largely avoid. Álvaro, Doña Paz, Cruz, and the other people whose lives I chronicle are already positioned within the war on drugs regardless of whether they work as narcos. In the stories that follow, we will see that those who become involved in the narco-economy do so precisely because the Mexican and U.S. governments have declared war against it. And as their stories show, for a long time this war was already being waged against them.

ONE

Narco-Wives, Beauty Queens, and a Mother's Bribes

When Andrés stepped out of his truck that day wearing his alligator boots, Isabella was instantly and powerfully attracted to him. She was eighteen years old and dreaming of living the opulent life of a narco-wife. I had never heard her say a word about the shy weed whacker until she saw him that day in the village, though she had apparently known him all her life. Soon thereafter, however, they were madly in love and virtually inseparable, despite everyone's disapproval. And then one day Andrés went out to work, like any other day, but didn't come home that night.

It was Paz, Andrés's devastated mother, who explained to me that he had been caught trying to smuggle a large shipment of drugs across the border. "It wasn't even his!" Paz emphasized, commenting on the intuitive injustice of the smuggler going to jail for getting caught with someone else's merchandise. And it was thus that Andrés was removed abruptly from Isabella's and Paz's everyday life. For Isabella, Paz, and Andrés's sister, Elsa, his sudden absence transformed their lives.

Media representations of the drug cartels and the war on drugs almost exclusively focus on men. They chronicle the exploits of macho drug capos, hit men, and smugglers. Music videos of corridos show tough-looking guys driving huge trucks and wielding AK-47s, often accompanied by busty, bejeweled, and beautiful women who appear backgrounded, as decoration. The drug wars in Mexico do indeed involve men most directly. Men are more likely to be lured into the trade (both to work as narcos and to work for the police and the military), and the deaths associated with narco-violence are overwhelmingly those of young men. The trope of the *valiente*, or brave, narcotrafficker permeates every aspect of the cultural sphere; the narcotrafficker is portrayed as fearless and violent in *telenovelas* (soap operas) and popular corridos, and this image is reinforced by media coverage of famous cartel bosses.

Nonetheless, my introduction to the ravages of the drug trade was through the travails and triumphs of women. Over the course of my research, there were several women in particular whose experiences were deeply revealing about the nature of the narco presence in the region and especially the way this presence is felt by women. But it was the women most immediately affected by Andrés's imprisonment who alerted me to the ways the narco-economy in the region makes women vulnerable. I had spent very little time with Andrés before he went to jail, but it was through his absence that I first came to know him. It was through the effect of his imprisonment on Andrés's family, particularly the women in his life, that his story became fascinating to me.

For this reason, I'm going to begin Andrés's story much in the way that I learned it and much as I approached my study of the drug trade generally, that is, from the edges. At the edges of

Andrés's imprisonment were his mother, sister, and girlfriend. And it was in the midst of the tremendous emotional and economic toll that his absence took on their lives that my role in this network of people began to develop.

The trajectory of research for this book was shaped by the fact that I began my fieldwork alone as a young, foreign woman and a stranger to locals. When I first arrived I had few connections among the people in local fishing villages. One effect of this was that it took me much longer to develop comfortable friendships or research rapport with men than women. This was frustrating because it made it difficult to learn about what life was like for local men and skewed my perspective on living conditions more generally.

My initial solution to this asymmetry in my research focus was to join whatever day labor projects were available where most of the local men worked. I volunteered in conservation *talleres* (workshops) and work programs on the river, like the one where I first met Andrés. While this did provide me with a unique perspective on the working conditions in such projects, ultimately it was not a productive strategy. The work was far too physically demanding for me, and later I realized the confusion that my participation on these work projects created. When I moved in with Ana's family in the village, a neighbor asked her if it was out of the same monetary desperation that led me to take these poorly paid manual jobs in the first place.

The reasons for these kinds of research barriers became clearer to me the longer I stayed in the area. It was Álvaro, the trafficker who confronted me about purportedly not being scared of him, who was most explicit about how my social status as a young foreign woman was perceived as odd to local people. On one of the first days I found myself in Álvaro's company, in the early stages of my fieldwork, I was sitting in his mother's house with his huge extended family. I had been interviewing his sister, a fisherwoman I'd become friendly with. I had met Álvaro a few times before, but for some reason on this occasion he asked me how old I was. I was twenty-six at the time, and I told him so. Apparently he had thought I was younger, so he overreacted to the news. "And you don't have a husband or kids yet?!" he asked, with not a little judgment in his tone.

Then I went on to explain that in Canada and the United States (I am a dual citizen of both countries) women often have children later in life or sometimes not at all. His sister and mother nodded supportively at my explanation, clearly uncomfortable with Álvaro's outburst. This only seemed to goad him further, and at a remarkable pace he started expounding on why that was ridiculous. "You are already twenty-six. And no kids! Think about it, if you have a kid now you'll be *una anciana* [an old woman] by the time the kid turns fifteen!"

Álvaro's comments helped clarify the ways that my solitary presence and lack of local family ties were initially peculiar to some people. Over time, however, people seemed to simply get used to me. In the process, most of the relationships I developed with male research subjects came about through the friendships I had initially established with their mothers, wives, and sisters. Living for stretches of time with Ana's and later Paz's family eventually allowed me to develop the kinds of fictive kinship relations that anthropologists often experience. For example, Cruz took on a fatherly role, and Javier and Andrés came to treat me as a sister. This was extremely important for my long-term research (as well as my general well-being) because it situated me within a social structure that allowed my presence to make more sense to local people.

Nonetheless, it was through my initial friendships with Paz, Ana, and Isabella that I began to notice the subtle but significant ways that the drug trade uniquely affects women. In this chapter, I explore how both the violence experienced by women as a result of the trade and the opportunities it provides are organized spatially in ways that are powerfully gendered. Because women in the north of Mexico often work from home they are affected differently from men and made vulnerable in specific ways by their presence in the domestic sphere. In addition, the social roles available for women in the drug trade, though diverse, contrast in significant ways with those available to men.

This chapter is about the women often obscured in coverage of the drug war: mothers, wives, and daughters waiting for their loved ones to serve out their prison sentences or trying to find justice for their deaths. But it is also about the women who aspire to another kind of life, the kind that is sometimes available to them only through men who work as narcos.

"WHAT ANY GOOD MOM WOULD DO": PRAYERS, TAMALES, AND BRIBES

I first met Paz after Andrés had already gone to jail, during the first year I lived in Mexico. I would sometimes wake to the sound of her horn as she cruised through the village in Andrés's truck, selling her homemade tamales out of her car window. Ana, the mother in the house where I was staying at the time, who was Paz's *comadre,* would often run out to buy some.[1] She would come back in muttering, "Pobrecita Paz" (Poor Paz). On those days, she would offer Paz's tamales around at breakfast. I could tell from their reception among the family that they were not the best quality. Javier, Ana's son, would complain the most. "Ma, why do you buy those tamales? They're disgusting." According to Javier, they were the worst tamales this side of the border—too mealy, and the chicken was always dry and tough. The only reason Paz was able to stay in business was because when she took them to the hunting camps the gringos would buy them. Apparently she even sold them to the gringos at a higher price than she charged the locals. But Ana would just respond to Javier's complaints by repeating herself, "Pobrecita Paz." The fact was that she bought them out of pity, and many other people felt the same way. I learned later that Paz's neighbor would buy some once in a while and then feed them to his dog.

I often accompanied Ana on her visits with Paz in Santa Ana. We would sit at her kitchen table for hours drinking instant coffee and nibbling stale *conchitas* (sugary breads). In truth, at first these visits were excruciatingly boring for me as the women talked mostly about people I did not know and memories I did not share. Santa Ana seemed remote from my research interests, which at the time were focused squarely on indigenous fishing rights in Ana's village. But I felt obliged to take Ana to visit Paz, and I spent my first few visits to her house impatiently awaiting our departure.[2] But Paz had such generosity of spirit and straightforward kindness that I quickly developed a strong affection for her and came to take much comfort in spending time with her on our visits. Slowly, I also became engrossed in her heartbreak and the sense of both chaos and fierce optimism she was experiencing during her son's imprisonment. She spoke often and dotingly of Andrés, who was featured prominently in the photos adorning the refrigerator and the walls. According to Paz, the day he went to jail was the first time he had become involved in smuggling, and it was just bad luck that he was caught. He was a good boy and had simply got drawn into a world that had overwhelmed him.

Ana's son Javier had also spent time in jail, and Ana and Paz's friendship crystallized around the shared experience of utter emotional suspension during their sons' prison sentences. Paz's situation was exacerbated by the fact that Andrés had gotten into a few bad fights when he first went to jail and, as a result, had made some enemies. At first he told Paz that it was an isolated incident, a squabble that got out of control. As the weeks went by, however, Paz found him looking increasingly swollen and bruised on her visits. Paz wandered through her days like a zombie. Between her weekly visits to the jail, she said she would lay awake at night imagining what was happening to Andrés, praying to Saint Jude (the patron saint of lost causes) that he was safe.

As her weekly visits continued, with Andrés bruised in an ever-increasing variety of shades, Paz started nagging him to talk to the guards about the beatings. She knew it was going to be difficult to convince him to do this. Andrés wouldn't want to snitch on the other inmates. But she kept begging him to do it anyway. Everything changed the day she went in to find that his knuckles had been smashed. He tried to play down the bandage around his hand, saying it was "nothing," but Paz panicked and tore it off to verify that, as she put it, "his hand was still there at all." She was horrified to find her boy's hand like that, and she started to get up, telling Andrés that she was going to go to the guards. Andrés stopped her and finally explained to his mother that it wouldn't do any good to talk to them. It was, in fact, a guard who had injured his hand. He admitted reluctantly that several weeks earlier, in what his sister Elsa later inferred would have been an alcohol-inspired moment of self-grandeur, he had "offended" a few of the guards. They had been giving him a hard time ever since.

Paz said that the world spun around her head for the rest of that visit, but when she said good-bye to Andrés, she resolved to do what she said in retrospect was what "any good mom would do." She marched right up to the guard on duty, firmly took his hand, and gave him a meaningful look. Then she thanked him for looking after her son. She released his hand, along with a wad of cash she had pressed into it, and as she walked out of the holding room she said, "Que Dios lo cuide" (God bless you).

Bribing guards is standard practice in Mexican prisons. By some estimates, guards can make millions of dollars a year providing basic perks to affluent inmates, and corruption in Mexican prisons regularly makes national headlines. One of the most famous cases was when Joaquín "Shorty" Guzmán, leader of the Sinaloa cartel, escaped from a maximum security prison in 2001 hidden in a laundry van. Guzmán reportedly paid "salaries" to prison officials of up to $4,500 a month, and over seventy guards were investigated for facilitating the escape.[3]

Most of the bribes to guards are made in smaller increments, to compensate for the lack of basic services such as adequate food and medical care. Mexico's prisons were built to house 185,000 inmates but now house more than 45,000 above that capacity, according to figures from the National Public Safety System.[4] Families often try to provide the funds to secure more consistent medical attention, to be able to bring in food, or to arrange conjugal visits.

Most of the time the cartels, or smaller gangs, buy protection for inmates. This is part of the taxation system that is calculated into the business of the trade, and gangs often have the resources to purchase such privileges for higher-level members. Paz, in contrast, did not have the resources to maintain such an arrangement. According to her, the cash she pressed into the guard's hand that day was all the money she had at that moment, and if the interaction had gone well, she knew that eventually she would need more to keep Andrés under the guard's protection. She was going to need to make more money.

Paz had been supporting herself and her family for a long time. Her husband, who was a fisherman and an alcoholic, had left when Andrés and Elsa were little. She had worked at a store for years and also as a seamstress to piece together a living. Then when Andrés was old enough he had helped out, first working odd jobs and as a fish cleaner and then getting into illicit forms of work. When Elsa married Rafael, their fishing brought in good money during the season, but once Elsa started having children the costs grew along with them. It was going to be hard for Paz to cobble together enough to live on by herself and at the same time make the money to keep Andrés safe.

That's why Paz started making and selling tamales. She would prepare the meat and filling the day before and then wake up at 4 A.M. to wrap and steam them. On one of my visits when I was staying on Paz's couch, I woke with her early one day to observe the elaborate preparation. She sorted through the cornhusks and piled the good ones together. Then she laid out the husks one by one, spreading the filling into their folds and piling in the rest of the ingredients: an olive, some meat, a slice of potato. Then she wrapped the extra husk around the back and at the end. Finally she tied little strips of husk around the whole tamal to keep the folds down. When she was finished with this meticulous work of wrapping and tying she steamed them. She had an hour and a half as they steamed to bathe, dress, and put on makeup, then help her grandkids, Celia and Kike, get up and get ready for school.

When the tamales had been in the steamer long enough she loaded them into Andrés's truck (which she shared with her daughter and son-in-law) and drove through all the nearby villages and a few of the hunting/tourist camps to sell them. She drove around with her signature stop-and-honk, lurching through the settlements and fishing villages. She made her rounds with a new batch of tamales at least twice a week. In this way she saved the money that she would take to the guards at the prison every week when she visited her son.

Paz often took the tamales that were left over after her day's rounds to Andrés's old boss and his boys who guarded a post in the desert where drugs were transferred. If she had sold all the tamales she would make them a batch of *tortas* (sandwiches). More than anything she just wanted to remind them that her son was still in jail, paying for their crimes, suffering for their profits. But she knew better than to communicate this in anything other than idle chitchat and offerings of food. They would even give her a minimal amount of money fairly regularly, and she saw this as irrefutable proof that they were going to get him out soon. But the months kept passing, and Andrés was still in jail.

WHAT COMES TO WOMEN AT HOME

The fact was that despite Paz's torment throughout Andrés's time in jail, we all knew she was lucky. She still had hope for her son. This was not true for Julia, who lived down the road from Paz. Julia had found her son dead, hanging from the rafters of their house, when she came home one afternoon. His death occurred under mysterious circumstances. The official story was that he committed suicide, but in several whispered asides I was informed that he was hung by his narco-bosses for failing to complete a series of tasks. No one really knew what had happened. But what was certain was that a few months earlier he had developed an addiction to crystal meth. It is often said that narcos don't last long in the business after they develop a serious drug addiction. They lose sight of their priorities, and they lose control. Julia also started smoking cristal a few months after her son's death. Now she spent most days sitting in front of her house, staring out at nothing in particular. Paz would sometimes bring her food, but I could tell it was painful for her to even pass Julia on the road.

For Paz, Julia's experiences were a reminder that things could be much worse. And for me, Julia's story was a first glimpse at the indelible loss that many women have encountered as a result of the narco-associated violence that has overtaken Mexico. I have met many women since who have also lost children to the war on drugs. For example, when I traveled with the Caravana de la Paz (Peace Caravan) in the United States in August 2012, I met Doña María Herrera, a woman from Michoacán who had lost four sons since 2008 (figure 2). They were in metal trading, and the first two disappeared on a business trip in 2008. Her family searched for them with no help from the authorities, and then in 2010, another two of her sons went missing. María and her remaining two sons are still looking for them, though they know the chances that they are alive are very slim. Human rights groups estimate that the number of "disappeared" could be as high as 25,000. Authorities are hesitant to even register them as missing, and they are rarely seen again.[5]

The principal way in which women are made vulnerable by the drug trade's grip on the region is through the loss of loved ones to jail or death as a result of their involvement in, or encounters with, the trade. Another way in which women are

Figure 2. Mexican mothers of missing children protest drug war policies in Los Angeles, California. Photo by author.

made vulnerable by their husband's or child's activities in the trade is through their presence at home. Often it is the woman who is at home when the army arrives to investigate a lead on her husband's or child's activities. In such cases, if a stash is found in the house the woman may end up serving years in prison while her husband remains free. Because many women in rural Mexico work from home, they tend to be at a greater risk of exposure. They are in the places where the police and military are most likely to search first.

On the other hand, women's positions in their homes also make them vulnerable to cartel coercion. It is not uncommon in the rural north for narcos to intimidate people into allowing their homes to serve as "stash houses" for drugs between deliveries or sales. In this case, someone knocks on the door and asks the woman at home to take care of something, a package, a vehicle, or a box. She knows from their clothes and the vehicles they are driving that it would be unwise to refuse.

Most of the stories people told of such occurrences involve someone the women recognize through a personal connection. For instance, Paz recalled that one time Andrés's old boss arrived and asked her for a "favor," wanting to leave some packages in her house for a few days. It was right after Andrés had gone to jail, and Paz felt that she had to say yes, for she thought that maybe it was a test of her loyalty.

She knew his old boss personally; they called him "El Gordo" (presumably because he was a chubby short guy). During the first few months that Andrés was in jail, when she still had hope that El Gordo would be getting him out, Paz fixated on endearing herself to him. She fed and flattered him endlessly. Many thought her efforts were misguided. From all appearances, El Gordo was not a high-ranking boss (as Elsa pointed out, the fact that he guarded his own trade-off post was one indication of his underling status). But he was Paz's principal contact and her only hope, so she treated him like a godfather, a capo.

Andrés's employers had been promising that he would not be in jail long, and it was not uncommon to hear of narcos getting bribed out of jail by their employers. She said she felt pressured because Andrés's release seemed imminent. And El Gordo had come and asked to leave the stuff himself. So she agreed, and that night a few guys dropped off a bunch of packages. She kept them that night, the next day, and another night before different men came to pick them up. She was so nervous that she did not sleep for a single second while those packages were under her roof. According to her daughter, Paz's condition was evident to El Gordo when he came by for a visit a few days later. He gave her a couple hundred dollars. Elsa teased that she had been so nervous that El Gordo could probably tell she was a liability. He never asked her for that kind of favor again.

A year or so later, with Andrés still in jail, a similar incident took place one night when I was staying in Paz's house. I woke up around 2 A.M. to the sound of two huge trucks pulling into her driveway. Paz went out in pajamas with a blanket wrapped around her to see what was going on. She talked to the men briefly before coming back in. She said that they were friends of Andrés and were looking for him. We both thought that was strange, as Andrés had been in jail a year at this time. "Why hadn't they known?" she asked herself out loud. When she told them that Andrés was in jail they asked if they could leave one of the trucks there until the next day. She said no, making up an excuse about how there would be men there in the morning fixing her son-in-law's fishing nets. After Paz had finished explaining to me what was going on, the men had still not moved their trucks. In fact, they were still out there talking, engines running. We sat in the dark, nervously peering out the kitchen window, waiting. Finally the men got into the trucks and drove away. Paz said she never saw the men again. A few months later she told me that an elderly woman, a friend of the family, was busted for running a stash house just down the street in the village. When Paz told me this, she made the sign of the cross and shook her head.

NARCO-WIVES AND BEAUTY QUEENS

When women are portrayed in the coverage on the so-called drug wars, the roles they play are limited. The image of the mother searching out information on a murdered or missing child sometimes emerges in coverage of the violence in Mexico. But this is a role that is rarely emphasized. Instead, the media tend to play down the extent to which deaths go uninvestigated. The role that is most often highlighted for women is that of the decadent, beautiful, young narco-wife. Tales of the women of wealthy drug traffickers lounging in beauty salons in designer clothes while having crystals glued to their fingernails are a consistent feature of borderland representations of the lifestyles of narcos.

I never met a narco-wife in this league. Those women I knew whose partners were minor narcos lived in conditions that could not be further from those portrayed in telenovelas, music, and the media. The families of lower-level male smugglers and traffickers live in a permanent state of economic uncertainty. For the most part, the women are left to fend for themselves and their children alone, if not because they are widowed, then because they are stranded without their husbands' income or paying off their debts while the men are in prison.

However, through my friendship with Isabella, I gained an appreciation for the dynamics that would lead young women to aspire to the role of the narco-wife, despite these local realities. When Andrés first went to jail, Isabella was devastated and devoted to visiting him every week with Paz. But as the months passed, she lost interest and eventually stopped visiting, and she started seeing other men. Paz could not forgive Isabella for this, especially because of the enthusiasm with which she pursued other men. She became the focus of intense scorn from Paz and her sisters, although she was able to maintain her friendship with Elsa, who always made a point of not taking sides in other people's conflicts. Paz said that Andrés didn't talk about it, but she could see the effects of Isabella's abandonment on him.

Narcos are attractive to many young women because they are powerful and often have money. They also have a subversive and rebellious persona that fits the cultural prototype of the classic "bad boy." Powerful capos often even reach celebrity heartthrob status, a fact that I was reminded of recently by a flurry of postings on Facebook by my young female friends in Mexico. They were posting and reposting a photo of Vicente Zambada Niebla, alias El Vicentillo, standing posed with his head held high after his capture in 2009, looking handsome, fashionable, and defiant (figure 3). Zambada is one of the Sinaloa cartel's leaders. He is still in U.S. custody as his case goes to trial in Chicago. His trial was not the important thing for my fifteen-year-old friend Arelia, however. She simply commented on the photo she posted with a heart shape.

One day, at my urging, Isabella tried to explain to me why narcotraffickers are so attractive. She told me a story about one afternoon in Mexicali when a handful of women were getting their hair done in a beauty parlor. One of the wealthy patrons

Figure 3. Capture of a Mexican narcotrafficker. AP Photos.

from a respectable family began publicly lecturing a younger patron who was known to be married to a trafficker. The narco-wife responded by ordering the hairdresser to shave the first woman's head. Terrified at the prospect of displeasing her, the hairdresser obeyed and quickly shaved off the woman's carefully coiffed hairdo.

Although it was unlikely that Isabella would have occasion to patronize a beauty parlor in the city, I assumed she knew the people she was describing when she first related this story. She told the tale as if she had been sitting right there in the parlor. Since then, however, I have heard renditions of this tale from several other people. That the story has circulated widely enough in northern Mexico to reach the status of an urban legend is indicative of how evocatively it highlights important aspects of the social role of the narco-wife.

Foremost, the story shows vividly how narco-wives thwart conventional means of achieving social status. This is brought out by the juxtaposition of the woman from a good family, wealthy by "legitimate" means, and the narco-wife, who is scorned for being complicit in an illegal business deplored by bourgeois society. The foiling of conventional routes toward upward mobility is even more powerfully underscored by the fact that ultimately it does not matter how "good" a family the first woman is from or how rich she is. Her class status is suddenly irrelevant. Nor does it matter how shallow and unmannered the narco-wife is or how likely it is she will eventually be imprisoned for complicity in her husband's crimes. It does not matter because, at that moment in the beauty parlor, despite the stigma attached to the narco-wife, the hairdresser shaves the upper-class woman's head without hesitation. The narco-wife is unequivocally more powerful because her presence evokes the power of the narco to generate punitive violence against those who disobey.

The story also highlights the ways that being involved in the trade in the deeply feminized role of the narco-wife is seen as a status symbol of its own, distinct from the symbolic capital available to smugglers and, to a greater extent, traffickers. The role is empowering in very different ways from the other roles available to men or other women in the trade. For instance, becoming a smuggler or dealer may afford women economic independence. But the cultural cachet plays out differently in that the power draws on masculinized traits of bravado. The risks are also different. Many of the wives of high-profile capos have had their heads cut off and have been horribly tortured and murdered as acts of vengeance on the part of their spouses' rivals. Others have been arrested and sentenced along with their partners.

One of the most famous of these cases was Miss Sinaloa's arrest with her smuggler boyfriend when they were found in a truck full of guns and cash in December 2008. The next day photos carpeted the newspapers of the beauty queen, Laura Zuniga, shown in a lineup for the press along with several unidentified gunmen (figure 4). Her head was bowed as she posed, shamed, in a simple gray cardigan, the glitter of Chanel earrings just visible through her cascading dark hair.

There is a noteworthy contrast between the photos of Laura Zuniga and Vicente Zambada Niebla in the same scenario. Vicente's head is held high, with all of his power retained in that moment, even though it documents his own capture. Laura, on the other hand, is disgraced. Unlike her companions, she cannot face the camera. It may not have been unladylike for the beauty queen to be cavorting with narcos. But to be arrested with drugs and firearms and implicated in those activities changed the symbolic connotations of her narco-association. While narcos are still narcos when imprisoned, the luxurious life of a narco-wife is compromised beyond recognition.

But for the most part Isabella's imaginings of what her life might be like as a narco-wife did not linger on the unfortunate fates of Laura Zuniga and others like her. Her picture of what would be in store for her stayed back in the beauty parlor. Isabella was ambitious and unwilling to settle for the kind of life

Figure 4. Arrest of a Mexican beauty queen. AP Photos.

that would be available to her in the village. She said that what she wanted was her own house and a nice car and nice clothes. One might assume that these are common aspirations for a young girl. But for a young girl from a fishing village in rural Mexico, they were dreams that seemed unrealistic.

Upward mobility for women with the financial and educational resources at Isabella's disposal is very limited. Therefore, more often than not Isabella's ambitions were more closely intertwined with romantic pursuits, and after Andrés's imprisonment her dreams were temporarily thwarted. After Andrés went to jail, she often talked about ways she could make the money herself to obtain the kind of life she wanted. Sometimes she talked about training to be an aesthetician and opening her own beauty parlor in Mexicali. But Isabella also often spoke of how much more difficult it was for women from the region to find work without an education. "Women can only work in the factories!" she would complain.

The factories to which she referred—maquiladoras—have been operating in Mexico for several decades, and, as Isabella pointed out, they are one of the major sources of work that exist for women outside of the home.[6] The dangers of working in the drug trade need to be put in this context, for the maquiladoras have been associated with another terrifying surge of violence that has specifically targeted women in the region. The femicide that since 2000 has claimed the lives of more than 3,800 women and girls particularly in and around Ciudad Juárez (with another 3,000 still reported missing) is a backdrop to what is often called "drug violence." Since the 1990s, many of the women who have been found dead, tortured, and raped in the desert outskirts of Ciudad Juárez were eventually identified as workers in the export factories (Wright 2011).

Both working in the drug trade and working in the maquiladoras, the main economic alternatives for women, carry large risks. But working in the factories has been associated with violence aimed specifically at women.[7] It has also been associated with extremely poor working conditions. Indeed, Isabella had worked in a glass factory in Mexicali for several weeks but hated it. The pay was terrible, the commute was long, and she was eventually let go. Like many of the women I interviewed in other fishing villages, Isabella found the work in the factories demoralizing and exploitative (Muehlmann 2013).

Through her boyfriends after Andrés's imprisonment, Isabella developed an array of informal strategies to garner an income. At one time she had two men simultaneously convinced that she was pregnant, and she demanded money from both for medical appointments or cell phone credit. There were several times when this income-earning strategy seemed on the verge of collapse: an actual pregnancy scare, for instance, or the possibility that one alleged father might have a revealing conversation with the other.

On one occasion, she tracked me down with a crisis that had emerged with one of her narco boyfriends. She explained, panicking, that she had "a package" she had to take to Mexicali. They would come after her if she did not deliver it that same night. She had had it for a while and had been too scared to follow through with the delivery. She kept imagining getting caught and had changed her mind. She did not want to go through with it anymore. She explained that the friends who offered her the job, her boyfriend and a few of the guys he knew, said they would pay her US$200 for a simple delivery just up to the city, not through the border (but presumably to a dealer).

At first she thought it was a lot of money for such a small package, but now she thought it was not worth it. She was too scared. But she knew that the reality was that not going through with it was more dangerous than making the delivery. They had been repeatedly calling her cell phone and threatening her. Her boyfriend was ignoring her calls. They said they would come to her family's house if she did not deliver the package. She said that the other problem was that she didn't have a ride. It occurred to me at this point that Isabella had come to me hoping that I would either convince her not to go through with the delivery or that I would offer her a ride—most likely the latter, something that I clearly could not do.

We talked in circles about the problem before Isabella finally thought of a potential solution. She realized that her mother and brother were waiting for a fish buyer named Don Emmanuel to arrive to purchase a load of fish. He would be taking the fish into Mexicali to sell later that night. Isabella thought she might be able to get a ride with Don Emmanuel. He was a kind man and often went out of his way to help her family. Isabella thought he would be happy to give her a ride.

Don Emmanuel, unlike many of the fish buyers that worked in the area (and there were many), was a trusted intermediary. Local fishing crews trusted him because he never reneged on preagreed prices and didn't just drop in and out of the village. He often stayed with a local family during the fishing season and sometimes even fronted families the cash to buy their fishing equipment. Many people told me that he cared about Santa Ana. He was also a very religious man. Some said he was a former priest, and part of what made his seasonal presence in Santa Ana salient was that he spent much of his free time lecturing locals and especially the youth about finding the "path of God."

He was most concerned about reaching wayward youth like Isabella. So, ironically, I thought, he may well see the long ride into the city as a welcome opportunity to influence her moral judgment.

I watched Isabella awkwardly emptying a bag of sanitary napkins and fit the package tightly into the bag. "In case we get pulled over," she explained. She was worried and said that maybe she should ask Don Emmanuel to drive "slowly," so that they would be less likely to be pulled over, but she didn't want to make him suspicious. It was unlikely that Don Emmanuel, who seemed a very patient man, would speed. I worried about being privy to Isabella's manipulation of this man, but I thought her plan was brilliant. And it had the added bonus that Don Emmanuel was a clean-cut, conservative-looking businessman. He drove a nondescript Honda Civic and had a self-assured religiosity about him that would make him even less suspicious if they were to be searched. Isabella smiled. "He'll never have to know what I'm carrying with me," she said. She started to calm down, confident in her new plan. Then we walked over to her uncle's house where everyone was waiting with the fish. I went back to Paz's, where I was staying, as they waited to make their fish deal. Many hours later, Isabella returned from Mexicali. She texted to say it was over. She was safe, and she was immensely relieved.

Months later, after Isabella had a few similar experiences, we talked about the incident again. I asked her why she had agreed to take the job in the first place. "I had to cross drugs out of necessity," she said. Then she went on in a self-justifying tone, "There are moments when you can't find money and you become desperate because you want to find money to help your family. And this moment arrived for me." My own impression at the time was that this opportunity had made itself available through her boyfriend and that it seemed like easy money. But Isabella understood or at least portrayed the incident strictly in terms of family obligation. She said, "I had to find work, I had to do something because I thought I had to support my home. And when they wouldn't give me work, I had to put myself to work in what I could." She portrayed her vulnerability as placing her actions firmly within structures of gender disadvantage, lack of education, and an economy that provided few opportunities.

I was struck by Isabella's construal of the events because her family did not depend on her, and she had never expressed a sense of financial responsibility for them in any other context. They were very poor, but her mother relied almost entirely on her son, a fisherman, for food, water, and electricity. This was noteworthy because Isabella never felt the need to justify her other methods of making money. Extorting small amounts of money from her lovers by lying about her pregnancy, for example, struck me as dangerous considering the men she dated. But she would often dismiss my worries that she might be putting herself at risk and had no qualms about deceiving her boyfriends for cash. She certainly never claimed to be doing it for the good of her family.

This highlighted that the meanings associated with women who get involved in smuggling are more overdetermined than they are for men. Indeed, none of the women I have met who worked as mules identified themselves as narcos or smugglers. The majority agreed to make a run only a handful of times, and usually in contexts they described as financially desperate. While Isabella's explanation did not seem to resonate with the details of her own situation, she drew on the social discourses available to account for women's involvement in the trade. While male involvement is about rational business opportunities and bravery, female smuggling or trafficking is often understood through the idiom of sacrifice for the family and particularly one's children. It also indicates that women's involvement requires more justification than men's so as not be perceived as morally reproachable.

Therefore, while Isabella was attracted to the figure of the unapologetically violent narco and claimed she would have been proud to take up the role of such a man's wife, she was, like many women I knew, uncomfortable portraying her own brush with the trade in a way that accorded her power or agency. This was because there were not sufficient symbolic resources locally available to positively interpret her involvement as anything other than self-sacrificing.

Women rarely volunteered stories such as this about their involvement in the drug trade unless I had a long-standing and close relationship with them. In my interviews on the topic, I never asked people directly if they had worked in some respect for the trade. But sometimes people volunteered stories in the context of questions about how they had been "affected" by the war on drugs. I came to recognize that women in general played down the extent of their own involvement or their families'. This is not surprising, due to the illicit nature of these activities, but it is in sharp contrast to the ways men were sometimes quite forthright about their involvement.

An incident that highlighted this juxtaposition occurred with the first family I lived with in Mexico. When I moved into Ana's house her son Javier had just gotten out of jail. Javier told me in one of our first conversations that he'd gone to jail because he was caught smuggling a load of drugs in his fishing boat. Ana told me on another occasion that he went to jail because he was caught in a stolen boat (not with drugs) that he hadn't known was stolen. Months later, I told her that Javier had told me about the drugs. I wanted her to know that I wasn't going to judge him, and I also thought she could relax if she didn't have to keep up the pretense. But she insisted that he had made that up. "Why would he make something like that up?" I asked. "Oh, he just wants to impress you," she explained. A year or so later, she adjusted the story. Now she said Javier had gone to jail because he was caught in a boat with a load of drugs he hadn't known was there. She said he was framed by the rest of the fishing crew. I wondered about that, but Javier just rolled his eyes when I tried to confirm the story. It wasn't until six years after I had met Ana that one night she told me about Javier's smuggling and arrest, finally admitting that her son had worked as a minor narco.

When women did talk openly about their family's involvement in the drug trade they tended to highlight the drastic financial circumstances that led their husbands or sons into the work. Alma, one of Paz's sisters, told me that one year things got so bad that she had to cut up their bedsheets and use them as diapers for the baby. Alma had cervical cancer and was undergoing expensive treatment, and her husband, José, collected and sold scrap metal and worked as a farmhand, but there wasn't enough work to meet their basic needs. So, without any sheets on the bed, Alma said she'd had enough and went to Álvaro, who was the primary narco contact in Santa Ana at the time, and asked if there was any work for José. Alma didn't want him getting into anything permanent; she just thought that maybe they could make enough money to cover the treatments and hold them over until she recovered. Álvaro suggested that he make just a few runs—not crossing any checkpoints or borders, which would be riskier and which he didn't think José was up for, but maybe some more-local transportation. Álvaro was able to find

José work, and since then, Alma said, they've had both sheets and diapers.

NARCO-QUEENS, NARCO-MOMS, AND
OTHER WOMEN AS BADASS AS MEN

The physical presence of women in homes makes them targets for both narcos and the military. At the same time, I've argued, their ideological place in the home, as the primary and often sole caregivers of children, excludes them from benefiting from the symbolic capital and prestige associated with the trade. Ultimately, however, it's from this division of gendered labor that another role for women has emerged amid the violence. Rather than "poor narco-moms," portrayed by the media as not even knowing what their kids were up to before they were killed, women who lose their children are increasingly taking a political stance. For example, during the Mexican Peace Caravan in the United States, I asked a woman I met, Areceli, if she didn't feel frightened to be on such a tour after the numerous death threats she had received since she began investigating her son's disappearance in 2009. She said that the threats are the only way she knows she's getting closer to the truth. She searches and searches, and sometimes a few months pass without a death threat. When she receives another threat, she takes it as a sign that she's on the right track.

The same self-sacrificing characteristics that render female involvement in the trade apologetic also create potential challenges for the network of cartel and government interests that attempt to prevent the investigation of murders and disappearances. This then is another role for women that emerges from the home: the unrelenting mothers who have nothing more to lose and will stop at nothing to trace what happened to their children and to demand accountability.[8] Though women make up a smaller proportion of murder victims in Mexico, they are the ones left to struggle in the wake of the violence. They are the ones left to bear witness and to demand justice, and they are also left to fend for their families under the same economic conditions that drew their husbands and sons into the trade in the first place. These are conditions that are permeated by social and economic networks that are intertwined with illegal actors.

The role of women in the drug trade in Mexico has been changing rapidly over the past few years. While Areceli, Paz, and Isabella were for the most part peripherally involved in illegal activities, more recently women in Mexico have become direct participants. They have been actively recruited by the cartels to work as burreros because they can more easily pass through military checkpoints and borders as security has increased. In fact, in the past few years there have been several cases of women in their sixties and seventies caught with large loads of cocaine and marijuana boarding planes and crossing military checkpoints in and around Mexicali.[9] Arturo Santamaría, a researcher at the Autonomous University of the State of Sinaloa, argues that more and more women are playing major roles in Mexico's underground drug world. This is due in part to the fact that the violence has claimed a large number of men in the borderland cities. According to Santamaría, in some cases a woman will take over the end of an operation when her father and brothers are killed. In other cases, they start by transporting drugs, laundering money, and engaging in "narcodiplomacy" and later get involved in larger-scale operations (Santamaría 2012). As of October 2011, Mexican authorities have identified forty-six female cartel leaders, according to the country's attorney general's office.[10] Because of this increased involvement there has also been a significant rise in the rates of women incarcerated in Mexico. A decade ago most women were in prison for theft or "crimes of passion," such as killing a spouse or lover. By 2009, the majority were incarcerated for crimes related to drug trafficking. And 80 percent of first-time female inmates were addicts or users.[11]

One question that emerges about women's varied involvement in the drug trade concerns what this ultimately means for their quality of life and levels of empowerment generally. Campbell (2005) argues that women's involvement and the effects of smuggling and trafficking on their lives vary depending on their social and class position as well as their place within drug organizations. He describes how women at the higher levels of the trade have found trafficking empowering in ways women occupying lower positions do not. He points out that women in higher positions sometimes adopt stylized capo roles or postures but use them for their own ends. Cameron Mark Edberg (2004b) also documents that female narcotraffickers are increasingly featured in northern Mexican folklore. The role of the powerful female capo is famously portrayed in Arturo Perez-Reverte's critically acclaimed novel, *The Queen of the South*, which was later made into a popular telenovela, about a young woman from Sinaloa who becomes the mastermind of a multimillion-dollar drug empire operating from southern Spain.[12] The late Jenni Rivera, who was the leading female narco-corrido artist in a genre otherwise dominated by men, personifies another adaptation of masculine norms in narco-culture. Jenni embodied the gendered transgression of norms as a Mexican American singer who had made a career exploring "vulgar" themes and an edgy "narco-chic" image: alligator skin boots and high-end cowgirl hats. Critics accused her of "coarsening Mexican femininity," but Jenni claimed that her intentions were more precise. Her message was simply that women "can be as badass as men."[13]

For women such as Paz, Isabella, and the others I've described here, the allure of powerful and legendary female figures such as Jenni and Teresa Mendoza shapes their experiences in the drug trade. But more important, their experiences are shaped by the immediate circumstances they are immersed in, which make the drug trade one of a limited set of strategies for survival. These strategies are constrained both by the risks involved in living and working in narco territory and by the meanings that shape their options. Women like Isabella and Paz confront the dilemma of doing dangerous and exploitative work at the maquiladoras or being vulnerable to state agents and the narcos. They are also confronted by their own attraction to the trade and to the men involved in it despite the contradictory impact it has on women's lives. More than anything, their experience with the drug trade is defined by the loss of sons and loved ones.

On one occasion Paz admitted that she knew she could never sell enough tamales to ensure Andrés's safety. She knew there weren't enough bribes in the world to console her as she tried to sleep at night, thinking about Andrés in jail. She realized that ultimately she was not in control of the situation. She could only wait and pray that Andrés would be okay and that he would soon be released. And she had faith that her prayers to Saint Jude would be enough. I asked why she prayed to Saint Jude. It seemed a strange choice of saints given her steadfast belief that Andrés would be okay, and her appeal to Saint Jude seemed fit for the bleakest of possible outcomes, that is, lost or impossible causes. But Paz explained that Saint Jude is not the saint to appeal to when you have lost hope. To the contrary, he's the saint you appeal to when you have no other options. He's the saint you pray to as a last resort. It was natural to turn to this saint during the long nights as she wondered what was happening to Andrés in jail.

TWO

"When I Wear My Alligator Boots"

All of Santa Ana was alive with anticipation when the news came that Andrés was finally getting out of jail. Paz cooked for days in preparation for his return, and on his first night home he was welcomed like a celebrity. His cousins, neighbors, aunts, and uncles gathered around makeshift tables and chairs in front of Paz's house. Many people brought food and beer and sang along with corridos all night. Even Isabella and her mother came to welcome him. By the end of the night, Andrés was back in Isabella's embrace. In a cloud of desert dust, they danced closely to corrido after corrido late into the night.

But the next day, Andrés had to start coming to terms with a life he thought he had left behind years ago. He began working low-paid odd jobs again. For a few weeks, he hauled rocks for various municipal road improvement projects. He said this was the way he wanted it. He wanted to start a new life. He wanted to get "out." It was Andrés's experience adjusting to life as a former narcotraficante that first drew my attention to the immense prestige and cultural capital this role confers on men. When

Andrés got out of jail, he vowed he would not get involved with the mafia again. After what was by all accounts a traumatic time in prison, he realized that it was far too dangerous a job to be worthwhile. But he struggled with the transition in ways that revealed how the trade becomes appealing to some men.

The common explanation for the appeal of the narco-economy among the population on the Mexican border is economic (Malkin 2001). It is very difficult to get data on this due to the illicit nature of the trade, but by some estimates the drug trade in Mexico brings in $30 billion in revenue annually, or 3 to 4 percent of Mexico's gross domestic product.[1] On the border, where economic opportunities are limited, the trade offers low-level employment that pays significantly more than legal work. It also produces revenue for more than two hundred thousand farmers and generates jobs in the transportation, security, banking, and communications sectors. For locals in this region, smuggling has become an attractive alternative to social and economic marginalization.

Andrés felt a tremendous amount of guilt for having left his mother alone for so long while he was in jail, and on his return home he was newly attentive to how he could be helpful to her. If he saw her go out to the spigot to haul water in for the dishes he would rush out to bring in the water himself. He gave her most of his wages for the household, working overtime in order to do so. Much like Paz, he seemed tireless. He was up at 5 A.M. every day to work nine to ten hours in the blistering sun. He never complained about the work. He did, however, talk about his lower status and his tremendously lower pay. This clearly weighed heavily on him. He said he felt like all he did was take orders all day.

Watching Andrés readjust to the drudgery of the work available to him legally made evident the economic rationale for working in the drug trade. This became clearer once Paz had to find new work. She was no longer selling tamales (sales had been less successful after Andrés got out of jail). Paz had gotten a new job in a nearby gringo hunting camp and trailer park. She was taking care of an old man whom she called *el viejito* (the little old guy) who was almost entirely incapacitated. For US$15 day—a huge wage for the region—she was responsible for feeding him and changing his diapers. Paz said that el viejito's ex-wife, who was staying in the trailer right next to his with her boyfriend, had arranged for his care. According to Paz, the wife and her boyfriend were meth addicts, and the husband, whose cash they seemed to be spending, was just a sweet old man. Paz was thrilled to have a well-paying job and spent all day between visits to the trailer and work at home preparing the old man's food. Andrés was devastated that his mother had to work (that she was making much more money than he was must have exacerbated the situation). He often talked about how he never allowed his mother to work when he was a narco, and he said he felt ashamed. He couldn't believe she was working "changing a gringo's diapers."

Andrés's experiences also exemplified how the trade represents an alternative to the exploitation and alienation many people experience in the legal market. But for Andrés, with several years of his life lost to jail, the risk of the work—the possibility of getting caught again—seemed to outweigh these incentives. He said that although he knew he could earn in one day what would take him months to earn as a contract laborer, it still wasn't worth it. It was his new awareness of the risks involved that strengthened his resolve to resist the temptation to go to El Gordo or Álvaro or any number of people he knew for work.

The vulnerabilities that Andrés now recognized were inherent to the role of the mule are in part due to the fact that the

illegal drug trade in Mexico involves a great deal of specializa-
tion and separation of sectors (Perramond 2004). The largest
and most powerful traffickers structure their operations verti-
cally so that the violence resulting from the drug wars hits the
bottom of the industry. The quintessential rule for the powerful
members of these organizations is to put as much distance
between themselves and their product as possible. Using mules
to transport drugs is one of the ways this distance is achieved, as
it is the mules who risk arrest.

Ironically, the strategy of reducing risk by putting distance
between the higher-level owners of the product and the low-
ranking smugglers of the product was also taken up in an inverse
logic that some mules reassured themselves with. Specifically,
because the product they were transporting did not belong to
them, they imagined they were at reduced risk of punishment if
caught. This was the logic with which Andrés purportedly con-
soled himself and his mother when he was in jail. Paz had
repeated this on several occasions, saying that Andrés's bosses
would take responsibility or that Andrés would be released
sooner since the load "wasn't even his."

However, the instability that people experience working as
mules is not simply a result of the risk of getting caught, but is
also, and most important, a symptom of the expendability of
their labor. Octavio, who was in his forties when I interviewed
him, described the many times that he was ripped off by his
employers after completing a delivery. On one occasion, a
cross-border trip to Los Angeles, he was supposed to make
$5,000 but in the end earned only $1,500. He said the bosses
took the rest. But he never actually met any of the "bosses"
because, he said, "they just send an assistant [ayudante] who
sends an assistant who sends an assistant. You never even meet

the boss or see him, so he never gets caught. Only the assistants get caught."

This description was revealing of how many people in rural communities that lie on trafficking routes actually experience the drug trade on a daily basis (figure 5). Many of the people I interviewed used generic terms such as *narcos, mafiosos,* or *la mafia* to refer to the individual gang members or gangs they had interacted with. Because the majority of people who work for the trade are low ranking, sometimes they are not even aware of which "cartel" they are working for.[2] People's stories often underscored the sense that one was working for an anonymous middleman and that one never really knew who the boss was. From their perspectives, the organizational aspect of the illegal drug trade appeared inchoate.

The opacity of the mafia's upper echelons to which Octavio also refers further limits their accountability to lower-level workers. Octavio's frustration over the risk he took for ultimately insufficient compensation also highlights the routine exploitation to which the lower-level participants in the drug trade are subjected. When I asked Andrés whether he had ever been paid less than promised for a run, he said it was very common. He said one would get paid less because there are often many bribes that have to be paid to get the load from the supplier to the mule, including bribes to ensure safe passage through a border checkpoint. So that is how the bosses usually justify cuts in pay: it's just "the economy."

The political scientist Peter Andreas has made a similar observation in his work on the history of smuggling on the U.S.-Mexico border. He argues that, in general, the rule is to buy off officials (rather than kill them, though this is also sometimes done). Thereby smugglers purchase a "key service monopolized

Figure 5. Rough route through narco-territory. Photo by author.

by the state: the non-enforcement of the law" (Andreas 2009: 23). Some estimate that drug cartels spend more than a billion dollars a year just bribing municipal police.[3]

The way that low-level workers are exploited by the illegal drug trade is highlighted by the widespread impunity enjoyed by higher-level members of cartels as well as complicit government and military officials. Perhaps the most explicit expression of this impunity is the fact that some of the most powerful drug lords are not just on the loose but also some of the most well known celebrity figures in Mexico. For instance, "El Chapo" Guzmán, the notorious drug lord who heads the Sinaloa Cartel, has consistently made the Forbes list of most powerful people in the world in recent years. In February 2013 the Chicago Crime Commission and the DEA named Guzmán Chicago's Public Enemy #1 (a title held by Al Capone during Prohibition). Despite the $5 million bounty the U.S. State Department has placed on his head, he remains one of the most elusive criminals of all time.

MONEY, POWER, AND *WAY* BETTER CLOTHES

Despite the exploitative and violent conditions under which they work, many young men in the region are valorized for being part of the lower echelons of the drug trade. The lure of the trade became even more apparent as the sheen from Andrés's former profession began to wear off. Just a few weeks out of jail, his newly rekindled relationship with Isabella disintegrated. It was not entirely clear at first that it was not a mutual decision. For the first week or so, Andrés seemed unaffected, and aside from an occasional dismissive remark about Isabella, he maintained his routine of going to work, coming home and watching television, and hanging out with the young men in the neighborhood by the fence (which is where the guys tended to gather to talk and smoke cigarettes). When Isabella would show up to see Elsa and me, Andrés completely ignored her.

Then Isabella started spending time with the truck driver called El Chibo. He would stop up on the highway above Santa Ana and visit her on his runs north and south. The whole village could hear him arriving in his eighteen-wheeler with the dramatic diminuendo of the engine gearing down and huffing to a halt amid the screech of his brakes. It was around then that Andrés lost his disinterested demeanor and spiraled into despair. A series of weeks passed in which there were regular instances when Andrés lashed out in violent displays of drunkenness, picking random fights and wallowing in self-pity. This was a side of Andrés that I had never seen before, although his sister Elsa would often make reference to it. When Andrés drank, he entirely lost his self-possession and composure. He was aware of this, and when he was sober he would sometimes talk about how he wasn't going to drink anymore. He knew he got overly "aggressive." But aggressiveness was only part of it. He also became very sentimental.

I hadn't really gotten to know Andrés before this period of his life. But because of my friendship with Isabella, I was often left consoling Andrés when she abandoned us both. On one occasion, Elsa and I had to drag Andrés from the passenger door of El Chibo's rig from which he was trying to forcibly extract Isabella. Not long after, when Isabella and El Chibo had driven away and Elsa had stormed home in disgust, Andrés and I were left sitting against the fence in Santa Ana. It was at that point that Andrés broke down and started sobbing, clutching his beer to his chest. For a long time he just sat there sobbing. Eventually he started to talk.

It was the first time during those weeks that I had heard him articulate, in anything other than violent outbursts and loud sighs of self-loathing, how he was feeling about the situation. He said it wasn't just about Isabella. He felt like he would never be able to get a girlfriend now that he was no longer a narco. "Narcos have money and power and better clothes—*way* better clothes," he said. "But El Chibo's a truck driver," I replied, struggling to make sense of what his nostalgia for his work as a narco had to do with the details of his particular situation with Isabella. He looked at me, the first eye contact during the conversation. He said, exasperated, "You think that he's carting jalapeños across the border in that thing, don't you?" I noted the familiar combination of exasperation and pleasure he displayed at being the one to identify and highlight my ignorance of the omnipresent narco-underworld right before my eyes.

Andrés's nostalgia for the time he worked as a narco before he went to jail continued. This manifested in a fixation on the items he had bought during that time. While he no longer had money or "power," as he bemoaned, he still had some choice items of clothing. On several occasions he mentioned how much some item of clothing he was wearing cost him, an obvious reference to the times he had money. For instance, he loved his classic button-down striped shirt, which cost $100. Sometimes he still wore his Jesús Malverde pendant tucked under his shirt. His hand would unconsciously move to it even when he wasn't wearing it. He also wore his alligator boots when he dressed up.

Andrés would comment critically when we saw local young men dressed like narcos when they weren't "really" narcos. Some wore lizard-skin boots (a cheaper version of the alligator or ostrich boots) or big hats and wide belt buckles. Interestingly, by his account it was acceptable to dress like this if you had actually had some brush with the trade at some point in the past. For instance, Javier, Ana's son, wore alligator boots like a badge of his past smuggling work. Even though he had been working as a shrimper since his stint in jail, on special occasions he would still wear those boots. Javier himself had also elaborated the importance of the alligator boots for legitimating his past work with the mafia. He said that while you may see people dressed as cheros, the alligator boots are how you know if they are *really* narcotraficantes. His boots cost more than $200, a sum that only narcos can afford.

Andrés's judgments about legitimate forms of narco-culture extended to broader kinds of assessments, as he was often critical of other people I interviewed about the drug trade's effects. One of my main interlocutors on the subject was Andrés's brother-in-law, Rafa, Elsa's husband, who was from a slightly better off family that lived outside Sauzalito. Rafa loved corridos, and I would often talk to him about music, corridos, and *corridistas*. Andrés thought that Rafa was a dork, *un pendejo*. He was a fisherman and had never had any real experience with the drug trade. He also thought I should not take Rafa's opinion about things like corrido music so seriously, commenting on a few occasions, "He doesn't know anything."

Like all formations of cultural identity, narco-culture has a history and is also in a process of metamorphosis. For example, the chero style, which was particularly popular when Andrés first got out of jail in 2007, references the classic rancher look and is one of the ways this persona indexes a rural past. But it is also more than a stylistic reference; it reflects the economic dynamics in northern rural Mexico by portraying the tough cowboy and survivor of rural adversity. One of the direct links between narcotrafficking and its rural roots was the fallout after

Figure 6. Icon of Jesús Malverde on rearview mirror. Photo by author.

the 1994 signing of NAFTA, which, as I discuss shortly, put many Mexican farmers out of business, and some turned to the cultivation of drugs and the drug trade as an alternative to the devastation imposed by U.S.-imposed neoliberalization (see Bowden and Aguilar 1998).

The "patron saint" Jesús Malverde, whose regalia many people in the region owned, also references a history of rural displacement (figure 6). The legend of Malverde originated at the beginning of the twentieth century in the state of Sinaloa, during the reign of Mexico's longest-running dictator, Porfirio Díaz (r. 1876–80 and 1884–1911). This period, known as the Porfiriato, was characterized by the influx of foreigners and advancement for the wealthy classes but increased poverty and hardship for the lowest classes. Malverde was a bandit who is popularly represented as having stolen from the rich and given to the poor before he was finally put to death in 1909. In the capital of Sinaloa, Culiacán, there is now a chapel dedicated to Malverde. He has gained a huge following in the north, where he is thought to have powers to protect and bless workers growing marijuana and smuggling cocaine. He has since gained a considerable following in the United States and Colombia. Significantly, Jesús Malverde is not just a "narco saint." He is recognized by many in both Mexico and the United States as a guardian of the poor, as "the Generous One" or "the Angel of the Poor."

Subtle stylistic and cultural differences such as the type of car someone drove, the saints they prayed to, the kind of shoes they wore, or the music they played offered a language easily read by local people, even if its meanings were contested. Andrés's and Javier's attention to what they considered contentious expressions of narco-culture was fascinating to me for a number of reasons. The way cultural identity is articulated and policed among different groups has been a long-standing interest in anthropology.[4] One of my own original research interests was how indigenous groups are defined and define themselves as distinct and, in the process, how ideas about what makes identities authentic are invoked in different contexts, such as speaking an indigenous language or fishing "like an indigenous person."[5] Andrés's and Javier's talk about what constituted a "real narco" was similar. Andrés agreed with the parallel between indigenous and narco identities when I suggested that they have a "culture." He teased, "We are your new tribe."

However, what is at stake in how indigenous identities are assessed seemed clearer to me at first. From within indigenous communities, what is at stake is often the passing on of what is understood to be tradition and a distinct identity. Among government officials and nongovernmental organizations (NGOs), what is at issue is often the allotment and distribution, as well as the denial, of indigenous rights (which is, of course, crucial for indigenous groups as well). But what is at stake in the strict delineation of how a real narco appears to others? It will take a few more chapters to adequately answer this question. But in the context of Andrés's transition, it was evident that his difficulties getting out of the trade were in part experienced as the partial loss of a claim to a cultural identity that had empowered him. His ability to make more discerning judgments than others about authentic narco-culture was a way of affirming his claim to that identity.

UNEMPLOYMENT AND PATRIARCHY IN CRISIS

Andrés's struggle to extract himself from the trade and his transition to working again as a low-paid day laborer revealed how powerfully he had identified with the role of the narco even if he was just an exploited smuggler. Working for El Gordo allowed him to feel that he was in control and to feel a sense of power and prestige gleaned from the cultural persona he had taken on. He understood much of his difficulties with his transition, his subordination at work, and his rejection by Isabella in direct relation to his fallen prestige.

His sense of fallen prestige was also linked to ideologies of masculinity that are bolstered by narco-culture. As many scholars and commentators have pointed out, narco-culture valorizes a particularly masculinized ideal of the "valiente" or "brave rooster" that taps into what is commonly referred to as *machismo,* a gender ideology already considered to be widespread in Mexican society. The *"hombre machista"* (macho man) is one of the most widely known cultural types associated with Mexico. Matthew Gutmann (1997), in his ethnography of working-class men in Mexico City, traces the stereotype of the macho man and how it has become ubiquitously linked to a "typically Mexican" macho. He argues that the Mexican man in this stereotype is represented as the undifferentiated category of the lower-class, hard-drinking sexist.[6]

The history of the concept of the macho in Mexico runs parallel to the emergence of the figure of the narcotraficante, and certain meanings associated with each are intertwined. While many authors have linked notions of the macho to the Spanish conquest of the Americas, Américo Paredes (2003) traces the concept to more recent historical origins, drawing connections between the advent of the notion of machismo and nationalism, racism, and international relations. Paredes shows, through an examination of Mexican folklore, that prior to the revolution the words *macho* and *machismo* were rarely used. It was not until the Mexican Revolution that a particular version of the macho man came to prominence. He links the inception of machismo to the rise of Mexican nationalism, accompanied by sentiments of distrust and inferiority vis-à-vis the United States. It was in this context, Paredes argues, that the Mexican male became associated with courage and linked to the machismo that became a nationalist symbol of Mexico.

Some social scientists have identified a so-called crisis of masculinity in Latin America (Gutmann 1993), which has been one of the impacts of economic and social restructuring in Mexico on the lives of men.[7] In the context of a deeply patriarchal order, in which men have traditionally been the sole providers of households, recent widespread unemployment and the recruitment of many women into factory work in the north has destabilized this system. Under the current economic conditions of the border, Andrés would never have been able to be the sole provider for his household through legal means, and this was part of the cultural context that made it so difficult for him when Paz had to start working in the gringo camp.

The economic restructuring that has affected men, especially in the border region, is directly linked to the economic and political relationship of Mexico and the United States. While the countries have a long history of interdependence, NAFTA profoundly transformed the dynamics of the border. On the one hand, it forced many farmers out of business by creating competition with agriculture markets in the United States that were much more highly subsidized than those in Mexico. As a result, many farmers were forced into the cities, where maquiladoras have been the preferred form of neoliberal development in the region. As discussed in chapter 1, factory work has primarily been the province of women (Wright 2011). NAFTA also created increased migration to the United States, prompted not only by a lack of jobs but also by a reduction in wages and fewer benefits in the few jobs left (Kopinak 1995; McDonald 2005).

While prohibition efforts have attempted to stop the flow of illegal products and people, the trade routes that have been opened up between the United States and Mexico have contributed to the rationale for an increased security and military presence. With heightened security protocols on the border, tensions have escalated significantly over the past few decades. Paredes (2003) argues that the marked antipathy on the part of many Mexicans to the United States goes back to the annexation of two-fifths of the Mexican nation to the United States during the U.S.-Mexican war (1846–48), which resulted in Mexico losing control of much of what is today the southwestern United States.[8]

Coupled with repeated U.S. economic and military incursions into Mexico since then that have undercut proclamations of respect for Mexican national sovereignty, an explosive dynamic has been created. The recent and intensifying tensions on the border and economic displacements since NAFTA have only increased the hostility of Mexicans toward the United States.

For this reason, many people portray the narco-economy as a deliberate and nationalistic response to U.S. power over Mexico. A number of people were explicit about this in my interviews. Cruz, Javier's father, pointed out the irony in the fact that while Mexicans and Mexican businesses are otherwise unwelcome in the United States, the drug economy defies trade restrictions and immigration laws. "It's the number one economy for Mexico with the U.S. There are no other businesses," he said. He highlighted the fact that agricultural subsidies made it impossible to sustain a viable market for Mexican exports in the United States and that immigration restrictions made it impossible to even cross the border: "You can't sell fruit or sell other things across the border. You can't even cross the border! So they are going to sell drugs." But it was Álvaro who put the subversive nature of Mexico's success in the drug export business most bluntly: "The U.S. is the boss of Mexico in everything, except for drugs."

PUFFERFISH, NARCOS, AND *CHINGONES*

Andrés's experiences entering the drug trade, being imprisoned, and attempting to extract himself from the trade after his release were shaped, not just by the hardships of living on the border in rural Mexico, but also by the legacies of political and economic marginalization and exploitation that frame the history of U.S.-Mexico relations. This legacy has driven prohibition policies as well as a parallel expansion of trade liberalization. It has also generated an entire repertoire of cultural forms, from dress and religious mythology to music. This cultural repertoire affected not just Andrés's consumer habits but also the way he felt and interpreted his transition from a low-level trafficker with sex appeal and money to a day laborer with, by his own account, nothing at all.

Despite his doubts, Andrés did eventually meet a young woman and start dating again. He had known Leticia for a long time. She was a few years younger than he was, from the nearby village of Sauzalito, and her parents had been friends of the family. For a brief period after he began seeing Leticia, life seemed to settle down for Andrés. She was a gentle person, and their relationship appeared to have a stabilizing effect on him. She was very different from Isabella: sweet and attractive in a delicate, understated way.

Several months after Andrés and Leticia became a couple, Isabella started telling people that she thought she was pregnant. Not surprisingly, no one believed her. A few weeks later she confirmed the news. She was eight weeks pregnant and said that Andrés was the father. Leticia was livid. The timing would have meant that he had been unfaithful, but Andrés insisted it wasn't true. Paz defended him, saying this was the kind of thing Isabella would do to manipulate him. Andrés argued that the father was probably El Chibo, the truck driver, though it was obvious to everyone that El Chibo hadn't been coming around for months. But Leticia finally seemed to believe Andrés. She was, in fact, soon pregnant herself. Isabella's and Leticia's baby boys were born around the same time. Isabella continued to insist that her child was Andrés's. Andrés continued to deny that Isabella's baby was his. No one knew the truth, and none of us dared to ask Andrés himself.

Sometimes Isabella would stop by the house with the baby. While there was still palpable tension between her and Paz, and now between her and Leticia, she would come to visit Elsa and me. Isabella would sit comfortably in the house, cooing at the baby, and she seemed to laugh and talk louder than usual. Andrés refused to acknowledge her presence, and he and Leticia would often lock themselves and their baby in another room while she was there. One could hear them arguing softly, the sounds of their voices audible behind the door.

Isabella said she was totally uninterested in Andrés. In fact, she said she didn't think she was interested in men sexually anymore. She started dressing in more "masculine" ways: suspenders, tight jeans, and blouses that highlighted her full-figured body. She cut her hair short and sometimes wore a cowboy hat. She had always had a tough look, but she was cultivating it explicitly now, and at one point she declared herself *"lesbiana"* (lesbian). One might expect that a gay woman would abandon the heteronormative fantasies of an aspiring narco-wife. But it turned out that in narco-culture there was room for her new sexual identity. At the time, the telenovela *La Reina del Sur* (The Queen of the South) was immensely popular, and Isabella confessed that she had a crush on Paty O'Farrell, the elegant and openly gay business partner of Teresa Mendoza, the famous fictional narco-queen.

By Isabella's son's first birthday, he looked exactly like Andrés. Leticia became increasingly furious as she watched the boy grow into living proof of Andrés's infidelity. Finally she left Andrés and moved back in with her parents in Sauzalito. Meanwhile, to compound the stress of Andrés's situation during this time, El Gordo, Andrés's old narco-boss, started coming around again. He started asking Andrés for favors. But Andrés said he knew better than to get involved again. He was resolute in his decision to stay out of the drug trade, and he kept repeating that he didn't owe El Gordo anything. El Gordo had left him to rot in jail—serving almost his full sentence. But he was agitated by El Gordo's pressuring, and not long after he started hanging around, Andrés decided it was time to leave the village.

Eventually, Andrés moved quietly to stay with a cousin in San Luis Río Colorado, a nearby border city, where he got a job working in a restaurant. I saw Andrés several times over the years that he worked at the restaurant. He seemed more subdued and clean-cut. I never saw him wear his alligator boots again. In fact, just several years later, it seemed that his style and manner had changed markedly. His hair was buzzed, and he wore clean white tennis shoes and the knockoff designer clothes that had become quite popular in northern cities. I often wondered what the transition had been like for him; aside from his work as a smuggler, he had only worked odd jobs or as a fisherman. Paz said he had started off at the restaurant washing dishes but was now a chef. She was very proud.

On one of my visits to the area when Andrés happened to be in Santa Ana, I had the opportunity to ask him about his new life in San Luis Río Colorado. He said he had his own apartment, which was pretty basic but fairly inexpensive for the city. Although he didn't get paid much, it was enough to cover rent and take time off. He said that he worked in one of those restaurants where you can see the chefs working in the kitchen behind the bar. He was one of several assistant chefs who prepped food for the head chef. Andrés said that he was in charge of making most of the sauces.

I asked about his boss and coworkers, if they got along and whether the workers were treated well. Andrés had had such a hard time taking orders when he worked on the road crews that I wondered if things were easier with the head chef. "They don't bother me," he said. "They know better." When I asked what he meant by that, he sat up a little straighter and with a hard look on his face said, "Everyone is afraid of me." This was the kind of posturing that I hadn't seen in Andrés since before he was working in the restaurant.

It became increasingly clear that although Andrés no longer worked in the drug trade, his narco past and his attachment to that identity, especially his "toughness," continued to haunt him. This was highlighted in an interview we did around that time about his past.⁹ The interview was not informative, at least in the ways that I was expecting. On the spot, Andrés fell into what had become a familiar kind of posturing. For the most part, he provided a hugely romanticized account of his time working for the mafia. He began with a fairly straightforward description of what his responsibilities involved: running deliveries for his bosses and being sent to intimidate people—sometimes referred to as "narco-diplomacy." Then we talked about how much money he made: thousands of U.S. dollars a run and a weekly salary of a couple hundred dollars. He talked about the truck that he bought during that time, gifts for his mother (including a TV set), and, again, he talked about some of his prized items of clothing.

But his posturing became more pronounced when I asked about the kinds of violence he experienced in jail. He said that in the first few weeks he got into a series of fights but that one by one he kicked the shit out of every one of the *cabrones* (bastards) who threatened him. Eventually, not even the guards dared to mess with him. Everybody was afraid of him, he said.

Because I had heard Paz's version of Andrés's experience in jail, I was struck by the divergence. The fact that Andrés's mother had bought off the guards in order to stop them from abusing him would have been unbearably demoralizing for someone like Andrés. Indeed, it was possible that his mother had never told him that she had started bribing the guards. Perhaps he assumed that the guards thought better of what they were doing to him and stopped their abuse of their own accord. Another possibility is that they stopped their abuse of Andrés because he was tough and that this happened at around the same time Paz started bribing the guards.

In part, Andrés's attitude during the interview resulted from his adoption of the position of "the narco" in a much more self-conscious way than usual. I was interviewing him about what it was like to be a narco after all, so he was addressing the topic differently than when he would have described his experiences in the course of a more casual conversation. There isn't a lot of room for subtlety when it comes to being a narco. And, of course, a narco who needs his mother to protect him powerfully desta-bilizes this identity. So all the vulnerabilities and the sensitivity that Andrés expressed in the context of his life more generally were erased when I was interviewing him about what it was like to work as a smuggler and then be imprisoned.

The phenomenon whereby people simultaneously become defensive during an interview and inflate their own role is what Elizabeth Dunn (2007) has called the "pufferfish" syndrome. In some research contexts, this is identified as a distinct impedi-ment because it is thought to make it more difficult to see beyond the posturing to the interviewee's actual role. The very notion that one should work around the effect in an interview, however, assumes that in other circumstances there is a baseline sense of self-worth that represents a more objective "self" and that that is what the researcher should be attempting to access.

Yet my interview with Andrés ultimately highlighted one of the most important aspects of his experience: how working in the trade as a low-level narco made him feel and how it allowed him to see himself. What he was describing was what was so appealing to him about the job. It made him feel brave and powerful, and it made him feel like he was providing for his family. And, of course, it made him feel attractive. The anthropologist Clifford Geertz emphasized the importance of taking such self-representations seriously when he famously defined culture as "the stories we tell ourselves about ourselves" (1973: 448).

But it's important to note that the "pufferfish effect" is not just evoked in interview situations. Unlike women, who tend to downplay their involvement, men at the fringes of the economy regularly exaggerate their roles in the trade. Samuel, the self-identified child assassin, was the most obvious example of this. But another instance that was touched on in the introduction occurred when I was with Álvaro, Javier, and Andrés and Álvaro referred to all of them as "narcos." Álvaro was older, more powerful, and more connected to the trade, but it occurred to me at the time that Javier and Andrés would actually be more accurately described as burreros than narcos. While Andrés had done some small-time peddling of drugs to his friends and acquaintances, it was my understanding that, for the most part, he smuggled drugs and sometimes acted as a thug. And Javier only made a few runs on his boat before the coast guard caught him. But that night by the fence was clearly no moment to mince words. Álvaro's invocation of their shared identity was also a friendly gesture toward the other guys, who in other instances he referred to as *los chamacos* (kids), dismissing their small-time activities.

I should point out that Andrés certainly was not all pufferfish. There is no doubt that he was *bien chingón* (a badass). Younger boys in the village idolized him, and older men involved in the trade, such as Álvaro and El Gordo, respected him. There were many occasions when Andrés's behavior made this formidability evident. One of the most intimidating aspects of his personality was his fierce protectiveness toward his mother. The first time I witnessed this was the only time I met Eduardo, Andrés's father. He lived in Tijuana but came for the baptism of Andrés's sister's second child. Andrés was there for the event as well. There was a party afterward, and the *padrino* (godfather), a well-off neighbor and old friend of the family, had paid to rent a jukebox. Andrés's father was a big, friendly guy who seemed good-natured at first.

But as the sun set and the night wore on, Eduardo became visibly drunker and started to make disrespectful comments about Paz—first an aside here and there, emphasizing that he had "certainly never missed her cooking" as he polished off another of the burritos she had prepared. By the end of the night, Eduardo was yelling at Paz and Andrés was yelling at Eduardo. When Paz started to cry, Andrés attacked his father. He was enraged, railing on him with his fists. When it looked like he might kill Eduardo, Elsa and I tried to pull him off, but Andrés shoved us away. Eduardo was left unconscious. Days later Andrés apologized to Elsa and me for shoving us. He turned to me and explained, "I just can't stand to see my mother cry."

Andrés's confrontation with his father was characterized by a physical assertion of power through the use of violence as a punitive measure. It's clear how his behavior was implicitly guided by contemporary expectations about masculinity that are particularly strong among the rural working-class poor. As I've argued, the perceived capacity to fulfill these expectations is epitomized by the role of the narco. To be clear, I don't think that low-level narcos are necessarily more macho than other groups of men, either in Mexico or beyond. Instead, Andrés's experiences and the stories he tells about himself suggest that current expectations about masculinity in northern Mexico shape the way low-level narcos understand themselves and their role in the trade.

Andrés's experience of his transition out of the trade was not just connected to his personal shift back to being a day laborer and his thwarted desire to provide for his mother, but was linked up implicitly to a longer historical legacy. The shifting emotional states that defined Andrés's different engagements with the trade reveal how people are affected by the material circumstances that mark, in this case, the life of a lower-level narco: first the rise in prestige and sex appeal, then the trauma of suffering violence in jail over several years, and then the trauma of realizing that staying away from the trade diminished his capacity to support his family and feel worthy of respect.

For Andrés, these are not simply individual emotions that could be fully rationalized or made sense of, but affects generated at an inarticulate and personal level. His fallen prestige had a longer history than his own experience and a wider cultural resonance than the assortment of narco-related cultural forms examined thus far such as clothing, jewelry, and patron saints. I develop this point in the next chapter, which is about how people listen to and gesture with historical ballads about narcotraffickers, an even more explicit expression of the unarticulated salience of the historical contours traced above.

THREE

"A Narco without a Corrido Doesn't Exist"

"He killed at a very young age!" they belted out, singing along to the popular song playing on the stereo, "and for this he lived traumatized." With every word of the lyrics memorized, Andrés and Elsa accompanied the song, following the accordion-based polka rhythm in a slightly intoxicated display of musical revelry. The song we were all listening to was a popular narco-corrido by Gerardo Ortíz called "En Preparación" (In Preparation), which tells the life of Manuel Torres, aka "El Ondeado," a powerful figure in the Sinaloa Cartel.

As the song shifted into the first-person perspective of Torres, Andrés and Elsa, in near synchrony, gestured through his glorifying self-description. They slapped their chests as the character in the song described his bulletproof vest. They slapped their shoes when he mentioned his boots. "If you're no good for killing, you're good for getting killed," they shouted, pumping their fists in the air in time with the up-and-down rhythm of the guitar.

Andrés and Elsa's spirited sing-along to this ballad about drug trafficking was not an uncommon display. Narco-corridos, or drug ballads, are a genre of folk song that tells the stories of men and women working in the drug business on the border. Over the ten years that I've been conducting research in this area, I've seen men and women of all ages sing, dance, and gesture along with songs glorifying the lives and deeds of drug traffickers. On quite a few occasions, I have sung along myself.

For many onlookers, this effusive, upbeat music is a startling contrast to the increasingly brutal violence that has overtaken the region. The violence that has engulfed northern Mexico since 2006 often takes elaborate and ritualized forms that draw on the medium of the corpse as central to the semiotics of terror. On the morning of May 13, 2012, for example, forty-nine decapitated and dismembered bodies were found strewn across the highway to Reynosa in the northeastern state of Tamaulipas. This discovery came less than a week after eighteen dismembered corpses were found scattered over a highway in the western state of Jalisco.[1]

It seems paradoxical, then, that despite this widespread destruction and suffering, the figure of the narcotraficante often constitutes a positive symbolic resource for ordinary people. The figure of the narcotraficante is not just an actor criminalized by the state but also one that is often revered by local people. The cultural salience of the narcotraficante is perhaps best exemplified in the rise in popularity of narco-corridos like the one that Andrés and Elsa knew by heart. The perceived power of the songs is also attested to by government efforts to prohibit their distribution and performance.

The carnage that has characterized the war on drugs in northern Mexico is entangled with an emerging narco-culture that, as "En Preparación" shows, celebrates the violent capabilities of powerful actors in the drug trade. However, the notion that narco-corridos "cause" violence is misplaced, because it imposes a rationality of function and a singularity of meaning on the songs. Representations of violence in corridos create powerful affective responses in the context of widespread censorship. But rather than naturalize violence or desensitize the public to its horrors, corridos are locally understood to heighten awareness of the violence connected to the war on drugs.

NARCO-CORRIDOS AND LEGACIES OF
VIOLENCE IN THE BORDERLANDS

The narco-corrido with which I began this chapter embodies many of the central characteristics of the genre. It tells how Manuel Torres was initially traumatized by the murders he committed as a child but was eventually able to overcome this trauma. He ultimately rose to the status of a respected leader of his cartel. And now, the lyrics say, "nobody can stop him." There are hundreds of popular corridos such as this one. They describe the protagonists' rural and humble past, often beginning with a traumatic incident in which they experienced some injustice, narrating their rise to power, which invariably involves violence both perpetrated and survived, and ending with a description of how they are now revered and feared.

The Mexican corrido is often portrayed as a cultural form that registers events and subjects that state-controlled accounts do not (Villalobos and Ramírez-Pimienta 2004: 129).[2] It traditionally offers a different account, the popular view, of events and subjects that are misrepresented in official coverage.[3] Therefore, a common understanding of corridos is that they serve as a source of transparency. Some scholars have argued that the corrido's popularity lies in maintaining this ideal that it speaks *la pura verdad,* "the pure truth," and *la voz del pueblo,* "the voice of the people."[4]

Many corridos also present a particular interpretation of the drug trade, highlighting political and social conditions that create the opportunity for narcotrafficking. In addition, corridos emphasize the poverty from which many narcotraffickers emerge and underscore inequalities on the border. The most immediate characteristic of these songs for the unschooled listener, however, is that they almost always feature violence. In their most commercialized renditions, the violence is gratuitous and celebratory—peppered with the sound of machine guns firing and trucks revving their oversized engines. Because I spent my first few years in the area researching other themes, and was relatively inattentive to the prevalence of narco-culture, I was puzzled by the bloodiness of the lyrics of songs popular in the region.

On one occasion in particular, at a celebration for the Virgin of Guadalupe, which was attended by many of the small communities in the region, I commented on this to Andrés and Isabella, who were sitting across from me at the table (this was before Andrés went to jail). "All these songs seem to be about narcos," I said. There was a brief pause before Isabella started to laugh and Andrés leaned over and whispered impatiently, "That's because they *are* all about narcos." They explained that this was a genre of music in and of itself. The songs, they said, were mostly about famous narcos and cartel leaders, but lower-level bosses often commissioned songs to be written about themselves by local musicians. With a nod of his head Andrés pointed out an older, nicely dressed gentleman. He said that there was a song about him too.

What was noteworthy about the role of narco-corridos at this event was that they were clearly not considered inappropriate but were very much a part of customary festivities. This was despite the fact that the festival of Guadalupe is one of the most important saints' days in Mexico (Guadalupe is the country's patron saint). The festivities that night were held outdoors in an open lot, beside a carefully decorated altar to the Virgin that people were passing and paying respects to, leaving tokens and crossing themselves. Families sat around eating tacos and listening or dancing to the band. Older couples danced to the music, and even pious Don Emmanuel tapped his foot along to the rhythm.

In fact, the people I knew in the area found it equally puzzling that I was ignorant of this genre. "Seriously?! There's no mafia in Canada?" Javier asked, perplexed. He assumed that if there were no songs about narcos in Canada, that meant there were no narcos either. This was a reasonable conjecture, since narco-corridos have always coexisted with narcotrafficking. In fact, there is a saying in Mexico: "A narco without a corrido doesn't exist." In other words, the relative power of a narcotrafficker is measured by the existence of music narrating his or her story. A place without corridos therefore means, for Javier, a place without real narcos.

The popularity of these songs has been interpreted by scholars, journalists, and government officials in a variety of ways. Some have argued that they are a form of resistance to state corruption and the oppression of the local poor (Edberg 2004a; Wald 2002). Others have argued that they are a symbolic resource for healing the suffering on the border (e.g., McDowell 2000). Many claim that the songs are merely propaganda for the cartels (e.g., Campbell 2012) or, by contrast, a journalistic genre revealing the truth of events censored by the government (e.g., Quinones 2001).

Several years after I began fieldwork, I asked some of the people I was close to what it was that made the music so attractive. On one occasion, my friend Lupita and I were giving Rafa a ride into Mexicali to pick up his family's car, which was in the shop. A song blared out of the stereo as we drove: "He never tires of seeing blood. He lives on the edge of danger." We had been listening to Rafa's CDs of corridos for the past hour, and I was beginning to lose patience with the music. "Why does everyone like corridos so much?" I asked. Lupita answered first. "I *don't* like them," she said. "They are way too macho and violent. I like *música romántica* [romantic music]." Rafa disagreed: "I love them." Then he said, as if to justify himself, "But you do too! And even the kids love them."

Rafa continued with his analysis of the songs' appeal: "They get you excited, right?" Then he added, "They make me want to drink." I asked, "But why do they get you excited? Why would they make you feel good when they're so violent?" Rafa shrugged, "I don't know. It makes you feel powerful. It makes you feel *capáz* [capable]." We arrived at the auto shop on the outskirts of Mexicali and dropped Rafa off. Lupita moved up to the front seat. As we drove away, she turned up the volume as track 14 started to play, which did not surprise me because I knew it was her favorite. "You're such a liar," I teased. "You love corridos." She shrugged.

Lupita's stance seemed indicative of an ambivalence that some people, especially women, expressed when directly engaged on the topic of narco-corridos and their violent lyrics. This is particularly the case among the middle and upper classes, which have long expressed disdain for the genre (Wald 2002). But another dimension of the ambivalence is apparent among women more generally in relation to the violence expressed by the songs. Nonetheless, when Rafa mentioned that "even the kids" like the music, I assumed it was Celia, his seven-year-old daughter he was thinking of. She has a collection of narco-corridos but especially likes Jenni. A poster portraying Jenni as la Gran Señora (the Important Lady) hung on the wall beside Celia's bed.

However, a few days after this conversation with Rafa and Lupita, I discovered that Rafa may well have been thinking of any of the kids in Santa Ana. I was sitting in front of Rafa's family's house talking with him and his wife, Elsa, and a few of their neighbors. Four children, including their two, were huddled around Rafa's cell phone, watching a video that he had downloaded. It was a video of the group Rígido singing "6 Impactos" (6 Hits). Before the music starts the video has a long, dramatic prelude at the beginning of a shooting scene in a restaurant. In the scene, assassins come in and shoot a young man, who falls to the ground. The police arrive and inspect his body. As a police officer inspects the corpse, the music starts. The officer, by way of detailing the crime, mouths the lyrics as the song begins: "Six shots in the body of the boy." Just in time, the kids started singing along happily. The song continued, "Hooded assassins wanting to kill."

I took out my camera and started video recording the kids. Even four-year-old Lidia was singing the lyrics. "They know the words!" I exclaimed, glancing over at their parents, who were laughing. They seemed to think it was cute, and they were also clearly entertained by my reaction. After the kids finished watching the music video, they refocused their attention on my camera, still pointed at them, and wanted to pose for photos. One of them, Kike, ran to get a hunting rifle from the house. I looked up at his dad. "It's okay," his dad said to reassure me. "It's not loaded." Then Rafa turned the rifle right side up for the pose (Kike was holding it upside down). The kids posing with the gun looked sinister but also cute, and everyone was laughing.

In the midst of this, Celia ran into the house and returned with a pink pullover hoodie, a woolen one for the cold. She pulled it over her head to pose with the other kids who crowded in together for the camera like a little gang. I asked why she brought the hoodie, trying to decipher how much of the narco-violence the kids understand. "To make it look more real," she said, as if that should have been obvious. She adjusted the hoodie so that the pink pompom on top was balanced, and then she took the gun from Kike and looked back up for the camera with her eyes narrowed, glaring out under the mask. The other kids crowded around the gun, staring up at my camera.

There were several aspects of this incident that struck me as particularly revealing. Most evident was the degree to which the songs were treated by everyone around me as harmless and unremarkable. The children's enthusiasm for the music and their knowledge of the lyrics, as well as their general fascination with narcotraffickers, were not noteworthy to the parents. This was underscored by the way Rafa reassured me that the rifle Kike had wasn't loaded. Rafa assumed my discomfort indicated that I feared the kids would accidently shoot someone. But I knew Rafa never kept his hunting rifle loaded, so that hadn't even occurred to me. My reaction was simply to the symbolism of such small children holding a weapon in the political context of the border violence. For Rafa, the potential for real violence and the representation of it was much more distinct.

In attempting to understand the appeal of the songs for local people, scholars have often traced the genre of the narco-corrido to an older form of Mexican ballad, corridos that celebrated the heroes and social bandits of the 1910–20 Mexican Revolution.[5] In the current context of widespread drug-related violence, narcotraficantes have repositioned the old imaginings of the social bandit, adapting them to the economic and political conditions of the border. The long-term forms of domination organized by the tension between the United States and Mexico and between elite and subaltern actors within Mexico have turned the image of the narcotraficante into a subversive figure with tremendous agency and countercultural allure.

There is much in this interpretation that I think resonates with the experiences of many of the people whom I have come to know. In part, as explored in chapter 2, the cultural appeal of the figure of the narcotraficante is drawn from the way it explicitly challenges both the Mexican military occupation of the region and the U.S. dominance on the border. Locally, U.S. dominance has been experienced through increased immigration restrictions, the growing and primarily U.S.-owned manufacturing industry, and the visible presence of the U.S. Drug Enforcement Agency (DEA) in Mexico. Corridos, in their original form, arose from a common and generally favorable disposition toward individuals who disregarded the imposed legalities of state power on the border. Smugglers, illegal immigrants, and outlaws have been represented by corridos as an outgrowth of a shared situation of oppression and injustice. Arturo Ramírez (1990: 72) argues that these songs express a "confrontation between the hero and hostile Anglo-American forces."

This point made by Ramírez more than two decades ago is just as valid, or more valid, today. The social salience of the narcotraficante, in this account, is drawn from the way the figure indexes heroes such as Pancho Villa, a popular lower-class military leader of the Mexican Revolution, as well as legendary outlaws such as Joaquín Murrieta, a bandit in Baja California and Sonora. In other words, that the narcotraficante can paradoxically draw from the cultural allure of old revolutionary heroes indexes the generative power of legacies of violence that run historically deep in the U.S.-Mexico borderlands. Rafa articulated this sentiment bluntly when he said that he liked the songs because they made him feel powerful and able.

Yet more needs to be considered for a fuller understanding of the allure of the narco-world for children. Six-year-old Juan, whose family I lived next door to during part of the time I was in Mexico, provided some insight into this issue. On one occasion, I found Juan crying beside the house. He had tripped during a chase while playing the game *narcos y federales* (narcos and federal agents) with some other boys. This is a fairly common game that Juan and his older brothers would play (much like the North American "cowboys and Indians"). Juan was crying because he had skinned his knee but also because he had lost the chase. His brothers had run far ahead by the time I found him. After Juan composed himself a little, wiping his tears with his sleeve, he told me that he hated it that his older brothers always made him play a federal agent. When I asked why he hated it, he said, "Because the *federal* always loses."

I had seen these kids, as well as others, play narcos y federales many times. And while it is not entirely clear that the boys saw the narcotraffickers as the "good guys," it is almost always the case that in the game the federales fail to catch them. The federales, as Juan perceptively pointed out, "always lose." Children like Celia and Juan may not be aware of the details of their government's U.S.-backed war on drugs. In fact, it is quite likely that for Juan the difference between a narco and a federal is not that marked. But they are indeed aware, as anyone in this region is, that the war on drugs has not only failed to defeat the cartels but has also empowered them. The violence associated with narco-trafficking has increased exponentially since Calderón's militarization of the conflict. And many onlookers have pointed out that when the government's strategy of targeting high-profile members of particular cartels succeeds in taking out one narco boss, a power vacuum is created that is soon filled with even more violence, leading to brutal skirmishes over territory and the immediate replacement of the old powerful cartel leaders with new powerful cartel leaders.

A CONTINUUM OF VIOLENCE

My reaction to the sight of four- and seven-year-olds singing along to the gory lyrics of the corridos and posing so realistically as assassins was one of distinct discomfort. My reflex was to interpret their comfort and familiarity with these songs as an endorsement of the violence or worse, a warning that these kids might get pulled into the trade. Their parents did not seem to be working under these same assumptions. However, there has been heated discussion in Mexico about the corrupting influence of narco-corridos on youth. Over the past thirty years, as the genre has become increasingly popular, there have also been attempts that have grown more forceful in the past decade to ban narco-corridos (Astorga 2005).[6] The logic of censorship was very much along the lines of the logic that underpinned my own first reactions: the music creates even more violence.

The banning and censorship of narco-corridos assumes that the violence is, in part, culturally determined and that the songs celebrating the narco-world will convert more people to the trade. The national security spokesman Alejandro Poiré said that silencing the songs is a key part of Mexico's "cultural fight" against violence. "The rhythm they dance to is that of the violence that harms many families in Mexico," he wrote in a blog post on an official government website.[7] The idea that the violence has a rhythm, the same rhythm as the narco-corridos, is interesting because it points to the way that such cultural forms are viewed by some government officials as existing on a continuum with the violence, to the point of sharing the same "rhythm." Ultimately, I've come to think that this particular interpretation is a misrecognition of the relationship between the musical genre and the violence itself. But first, in order to further demonstrate and qualify the way the musical genre *is* connected to violence, I want to give an example of how narco-corridos have been censored not just by government actors, but by the cartels themselves.

DANCING TO THE RHYTHM OF VIOLENCE

The capacity of violence to create more violence can be seen in the way the narco-trade affects the corridistas who write and perform these songs. Gerardo Ortíz, the singer whose lyrics opened this chapter, is a contemporary favorite, but the cultural type of the corridista has been around since the 1970s. One of the original narco-corridistas was Chalino Sánchez, who was also one of the most well known and loved. The singer's success has often been attributed to his charisma and to his ability to model his own image on the archetype of the noble hero (Simonett 2006). Sánchez's legend began in 1992, when in the midst of a concert he was performing in Palm Springs, California, someone in the crowd attempted to assassinate him. Such acts of intimidation and violence have been known to happen occasionally when a band plays a corrido venerating a figure who is considered a rival by someone in the audience. Purportedly, Sánchez was challenged on several occasions by audience members wanting to test his persona as a valiente (Quinones 2001). In this case, however, and in keeping with the reputation Sánchez had built for himself, instead of fleeing the scene he pulled out his own gun and returned fire from the stage. He then leapt from the stage and ran through the crowd, firing at the assassin, who was later captured and imprisoned (Wald 2002).

Several months after this incident, Sánchez was found dead in a ditch in Culiacán, Sinaloa, shot twice in the back of the head. Since his death, hundreds of corridos have been composed in his memory, portraying him as a brave, determined, and sincere man, that is, as having the virtues of the corrido heroes he spent his career venerating (Simonett 2006: 7). Many people believe that Sánchez has had more corridos written about him than any other historical or contemporary figure, including Pancho Villa.

While Sánchez was perhaps the most famous, many corridistas have met the same fate. Since 2008 four corrido musicians have been killed by narcos enraged that their music celebrates their rivals rather than themselves. Indeed, just a few months ago Ortíz himself was attacked while returning from playing a gig. The assailants drove alongside his vehicle and opened fire, missing Ortíz but killing his driver and his agent. Ortíz told the media later that he would not comment on the incident for "obvious reasons."[8]

Popular narco-culture is not insulated from the bloodshed it chronicles. In some parts of northern Mexico, bands have refused to take requests to play corridos for fear that they might endanger themselves. This seems to be the case especially in areas where there is intense conflict between cartels over territory and competition between gangs. Besides musicians, street vendors playing music from portable stereos are similarly cautious about offending passersby.[9]

Ortíz's recent close brush with the violence of cartels as well as famous incidents such as Sánchez's public shootout demonstrate that the production and circulation of these songs are intertwined with the violence they narrate. But I would argue that they are not intertwined in the way that Poiré, the national security spokesman, was implying in his statement quoted above. Clearly Poiré intended his comments about the relationship between music and violence in Mexico to be taken much more specifically. He implied that there is not simply a relationship between both, but a relation of causality, a deterministic relationship between the music and the violence in which the determinism proceeds in precisely the latter direction: music generates violence. The implication is that by silencing that rhythm, the violence will come to a halt.

The metaphor of rhythm evokes the image of a couple dancing a corrido in a packed dance hall. They dance in an embrace, the man drawing his partner in with one hand and with the other his *caguama* (a 32-ounce bottle of beer common in the region), and then the band stops playing. Does the pair keep dancing? Of course not. They stop, looking up, confused, toward the band. When the couple realizes the band is not going to start up again, they will surely retreat to their table. This is, in short, the assumption underlying Poiré's call for censorship: without the music there is no "rhythm" to propel the violence.

Censorship, as "a key part of the cultural fight" against narco-violence, is imagined as having a similar effect. As the popularity of these songs has spread to some parts of the United States, in particular, Los Angeles, similar arguments have been made there. The L.A. journalist Francisco Reyes used the familiar metaphor of rhythm in his discussion of the popularity of corridos. He argued that Mexicans complain about the violence and blame a corrupt government but are only partly right to do so: "They will not take a look in the mirror, for they've decided they will continue dancing to the beat of hypocrisy."[10] By Reyes's account, ordinary people are partly at fault for the violence because they continue to listen to corridos.

The government demonization of this genre, however, has other, more political motivations as well. Although corrido musicians had experienced suppression and control by the government since as early as the 1970s, the censorship of corridos only became serious more recently, when bands began to release songs that directly implicated high-level officials in the drug business (Simonett 2006). Government entities and policies have increasingly been implicated in drug war violence and in cases of corruption. And in the context of the increasing awareness that prohibitionist policies are spectacularly ineffective, censorship of the genre is a way to limit the public visibility of this failure and of the way the war on drugs has also corrupted state agencies. It's important to note that the kinds of violent censorship to which musicians are subjected, by both the cartels and the officials, are very similar to what journalists in Mexico have experienced over the past decade (Corchado 2013). The discourse of prohibition, in other words, is not just about the censorship of music but also about a politics of negation and denial on the part of the government (Ochoa 2006).

Therefore, the discourses surrounding censorship both north and south of the border reinvoke the idea that "a narco without a corrido doesn't exist." On the surface, this argument follows a logic similar to Javier's when he assumed that the fact that there were no corridos in Canada meant that there were no narcos either. The pro-censorship argument is the reverse: if narco-corridos are no longer available to the public the narco-bosses they revere will not retain their power. But the logic of censorship differs from that of Javier on one crucial point: causality. Javier pointed to the indissoluble link between the music and the violence as a co-occurrence rather than a causal connection. The sentiment that a trafficker without a corrido doesn't exist does not mean that a narco will cease to exist when his corrido is no longer played on the radio but that the legitimacy and prestige of a narco are profoundly and indissolubly linked to the way his exploits are communicated and chronicled for a public.

Some authors have suggested that there is a significant class dimension to the public debate about corridos.[11] The journalist Elijah Wald (2002) has pointed out that while calls for censorship have come from both the right and the left of the political spectrum in Mexico, what is significant is that they are articulated by the middle and upper classes. Despite their recent commercial success, corridos are considered "poor people's music," and this is the main reason they are considered dangerous: the music is reaching exactly the people who would most likely be drawn into the drug business.

While the music may indeed bolster the positive image of narcotraffickers, the main factors that promote extreme violence are not songs but widespread conditions of poverty, the prohibition of trafficking, and the huge demand for drugs originating in the United States. But retracing the causes of narco-violence on the border to these structural conditions of poverty and inequality does not illuminate the subjective relationship between the violence in the borderlands and the appeal of the songs for the people most vulnerable to the violence: the borderland poor. Below I explore how people themselves experience the relationship between the music and their own understandings of violence.

"BECAUSE YOU HAVE TO KNOW IT'S REAL": SILENCE AND CENSORSHIP

After a few days of sporadic yet intense discussion about corridos, Rafa and Elsa insisted on showing me a video. We walked over to their neighbor's house with the DVD they wanted to play for me, as they did not have a player in their own house. I assumed it would be a music video like the one the children had been watching on Rafa's phone. But when they put the video into the DVD player, Rafa and Elsa, along with the neighbors, shooed the kids out of the room. The opening scene showed a room with a man sitting in a chair, gagged and with his hands tied behind his back, and staring at the camera. There were six hooded men standing behind him. He held a sign that read, "A message to our enemies."

"Wait. Is this real?" I asked. "What is this?" They all replied, "It's real." On the TV screen one of the masked men put a bag over the gagged man's head and then began to slowly and meticulously slit his throat. I instinctively covered my eyes with my hands. "Look! Look!" Elsa ordered. I did not look up, but I could hear that the gagged man was still breathing. I could hear his breath gurgling through the blood. "You have to look! This is where they cut through the bone," Elsa shouted. "Why are you making me watch this?" I yelled back, my eyes still covered (I could now hear them sawing through the bone). "Because it's real! You have to know that those songs are not just songs. It's real." They all kept shouting for me to watch until I finally looked up as the masked men on the TV screen finished sawing through the bone and lifted up the head.

Finally, the scene ended. The DVD moved on to show much less dramatic video clips: low-quality footage of shootouts and car chases filmed on cell phones and handheld cameras. These clips were interspersed with segments from TV news programs. There was no narration, no apparent overarching theme besides narco-related violence. It was simply a collection of raw video footage. As the lower-intensity footage continued in the background, we started to talk normally again, although the conversation was still tense. Elsa said, "That's why I don't like corridos. I mean, I like them. But you need to know that they tell true stories, and it's awful."

The subject of black market videos of the drug violence in Mexico, which have proliferated on the Internet over the past few years, is too large for me to address in full here. What I want to emphasize is the point my companions were trying to make specifically about corridos. When I asked about the video, Rafa explained that such videos are sold at roadside stalls everywhere in Tijuana and Mexicali. He said they're sold because the media doesn't cover that information. "People buy them because they want to know," he said. "They want to see what's happening."

These comments seem to bolster the view that corridos tell "la pura verdad." But this insight struck me as slightly different from the one advanced by scholars of corridos who have argued that the songs form part of a journalistic genre—documenting the news stories that do not make it into the press. When people said that corridos are "real" or "true," what they meant was not so much that the details of the lyrics were true but that the songs were important because they reflect a reality that is also documented visually on video.

The journalist John Gibler (2011) makes a related point in his exposé of the many silencing practices that cartels and the government have used to control the flow of information on the drug wars. He argues that while local people no longer have faith in the capacity of the state, the military, or the police to restore justice, they do, nonetheless, believe they have access to some forms of justice. They believe in the kind of justice that arises in the midst of impunity and censorship whereby "speaking and contributing to knowledge are forms of rebellion against silence and murder" (25). Gibler's comments echo those of anthropologists who have argued for the salience of testimony where societies censor the violence that is inflicted on individuals (Das 2003, 2007).

In this interpretation, the existence of corridos heightens awareness of the violence otherwise distorted or obscured by the government or by the cartels' own censorship practices. This contrasts with the classic mainstream theories on media that hold that representations of violence lead to desensitization.[12] On the latter view, the objectification of violence increases the capacity to inflict pain on others since representations of violence deaden awareness by increasing hyperstimulation.

Alan Klima cautions against deterministic accounts that look at media structures and their effects outside of their specific historical and material relationships. His book *The Funeral Casino* (2002) analyzes the use of images of death after the 1992 massacre of pro-democracy protesters by the army on the streets of Bangkok, known as "Black May." He describes how mass-mediated images of the violence recorded by protesters and ordinary people, such as photos and videos of the killings and of corpses and body parts on the streets, were marketed and circulated in the aftermath of the massacre and amid widespread state censorship. He argues that these images ended up constituting the most powerful resistance to national media control, eventually contributing significantly to the overthrow of the military dictatorship (Klima 2002: 142).

In both the Mexican and Thai examples of black market representations of violence, local consumers understood the market's proliferation to arise as a response to censorship. And in both cases there was a government attempt to cover up the scale and nature of the violence. There are significant differences between the Thai and Mexican cases as well. In the Mexican case, the censorship is not just exercised by the government. While journalists have been killed for reporting on government and military connections to narco-activities, they have also been killed by the cartels for revealing too much information about their operations or by offending the wrong people.

In Mexico, unlike the case of Black May, violent representations are not yet connected to a well-defined political movement. Instead they are connected to a public impulse to counter the mass silencing and affirm the affective reality of the terror ravaging the borderlands. Both cases, however, show that graphic representations of violence exert powerful social pressures in political situations despite the existence of direct and indirect codes of censorship. As Klima argues, the powerful potential of media circulation in these cases, far from desensitizing the public, is able to heighten awareness of violence and censorship.

ON THE GENERATIVE CAPACITIES OF VIOLENCE

One day I asked Celia about the relationship between the music and the appeal of the drug trade for youth such as herself. We were listening to Jenni's hit corrido "Los Ovarios" (The Ovaries), an unapologetically feminist account of what it is like to be a powerful female narco-boss, whose refrain is, "These are some big ovaries I bring with me." I asked Celia, "Why do you like Jenni? You don't want to be a narco-boss when you grow up, do you?" Celia looked at me with her eyes wide and paused. She seemed to be trying to trace the logic of my question. "No," she said, finally and decisively, as if she was slightly offended or at least a little surprised that I would draw such a conclusion. "I just like her."

I was struck by the series of expressions that registered on Celia's face after I asked if liking the songs meant that she wanted to be a female narco. At first she seemed confused, as if trying to simply grasp my train of thought. When she realized that I was concluding that she liked Jenni because she wanted to be the character Jenni was singing about, she seemed almost irritated, wrinkling up her nose.

Of course, I cannot be sure of what really passed through the mind of this seven-year-old girl. What I know is that while I watched her digest the implication of my question, I retraced my own logic and realized that I was making some assumptions that were not fair to her. "Yeah, I like her too," I admitted quickly. At that point, her father interrupted from the other room: "She's fat!" That was all he had to add. With Rafa's comment resounding with even more irrelevance and unfairness than my own question, Celia and I both rolled our eyes and put the matter to rest.

Jenni Rivera herself has had to answer questions about whether the music has a negative effect on youth. Many corridistas have dismissed these kinds of concerns. Directly arguing against such theories, Jenni Rivera said in an interview that she thought the music gives the listeners "an adrenaline rush; they get hyped up and it makes them happy. It makes them feel tough and it makes them feel, like, really, really Mexican. And I think we all like to feel like that" (quoted in Wald 2002: 144).

What is clear from the reactions and comments of people I've described here is that cultural production related to violence, such as the performance and consumption of narco-corridos, is not solely meaningful in relation to physical violence. The meanings such cultural forms produce for local people arise parallel and sometimes peripherally to actual instances of violence. It may be more useful to think about the generative capacity of violence in reference to these songs: its capacity not only to destroy but also to create.

The generative capacity of the narco-corrido is all the more striking given the destructiveness of drug addiction, which the songs rarely mention. The figure of the narcotraficante, the protagonist that emerges from the corrido genre, absorbs all the positive and celebratory associations of the drug trade. The power and triumph that come to be associated with the narcotraficante contrast powerfully with his anti-archetype: the tragic, hopeless addict. As I discuss in the next chapter, the figure of the addict is obscured almost entirely by the genre of the corrido. But the effects of drug addiction on the lives of local people is the backdrop of everyday life in northern rural Mexico.

FOUR

The View from Cruz's Throne

One day Paz asked if I would go with her to ask the gringos she was working for a few questions. She wanted me to translate. She said it was frustrating trying to communicate with *el viejito*, who could barely talk anyway. He would occasionally try to say something to Paz, and she had no idea what he was talking about. What if he didn't like something about the food? She wanted to ask Linda, the woman who had hired her, if everything was okay. So Andrés drove us there, and we pulled up to the largely vacant lot of trailer hookups. It was one of a half dozen tourist and hunting camps in the former riverbed of the Colorado delta that used to cater to a clientele of Americans and Mexicans. The tourism industry in the region has declined markedly as a result of drug-related violence and the drying up of the delta, which has taken a toll on the local ecosystem. The camp was now abandoned, except for the trailer and the motor home where Paz's employers were staying. Paz and I got out of the car, and Andrés stayed there to wait.

As we approached, I saw Linda emerge from the trailer, smiling and waving at Paz. She had big hair and pale blue eyes. I thought she was probably in her late fifties. She was extremely thin and dressed in a faded one-piece jumper. She gave us a warm reception, and after Paz introduced us she immediately started praising Paz. "Paz is my angel," she said, "Aren't you, Paz? Don't I always tell you you're my angel?" She was jittery and said the word again for Paz with a Spanish accent. "AN-HELL," she pronounced loudly and badly. Paz nodded to Linda in the exaggerated body language one often resorts to in difficult linguistic interactions. "Yes, that's what she always tells me," she confirmed to me (in Spanish). I told Linda that Paz was really happy working for them. Then Paz had me translate a few questions about el viejito's dietary preferences.

When Paz finished asking her questions, she took the containers of food she had brought to the old man. I stayed with Linda, curious to learn more about her and this arrangement she had with her husband and boyfriend. Linda didn't need much prompting. She said they were from Los Angeles but came to Mexico for most of the year because it was easier and cheaper to care for her husband—"the old man," she called him—here. She explained that they hadn't been together as a married couple for a long time. Her boyfriend, Greg, who she said was a "real asshole," lived with her now. Her husband had a bad stroke a few years back, on his sixty-second birthday. "The poor thing," she stammered, her eyes darting around. She explained that he was now almost completely debilitated. She said it had been exhausting caring for him. "But that's what you get for marrying a man twenty-five years older than you!"

She kept talking, but I stopped listening. I had tuned her out to do some calculations. If her husband was over 62 and she was 25 years younger, that put her in her early 40s, not her 50s as I had estimated. I stood there as she talked, completely absorbed in examining the incredible physical effects of meth addiction: her sunken eyes and ragged, loose skin. Finally, I was jarred out of my meditation on her face by the sound of her boyfriend yelling from the trailer, "Linda, where are my glasses!" "I don't know," she screamed back, pulling a pack of Marlboros out of her jumper pocket. "Linda!" he yelled again, louder this time, "Where the FUCK are my glasses!" Linda's face suddenly transformed into a snarl. "You asshole!!!" she screeched. Then she stood there glassy-eyed and drew hard on her cigarette. "I'm so sorry," she said. "Excuse me, but I have to go help him." She walked a little off balance toward the trailer where Greg was.

I turned toward the motor home where Paz was with the old man. She was calling me, saying he wanted to meet me. I walked in, immediately taken aback by the dank smell. The skinny old man was lying on a narrow bed, and Paz was feeding him soup from a container. He was very frail and seemed disoriented but raised his trembling hand to take mine and smiled sweetly. Paz wiped soup from his chin, smiling down at him in an encouraging way. I sat sideways on the driver's seat and looked around the motor home: it was heaped with garbage, empty packs of cigarettes, and old food. There was a pipe sitting by the driver's window and piles of paper all over the floor.

Paz started changing the old man's diaper. She was matter-of-fact as she gently but firmly maneuvered his body to remove his clothes. She looked just the way she did taking care of all her grandchildren, sweet and gentle and tireless. I got up to go out, feeling uncomfortable watching but also ready to escape the stench of the trailer. As I reached the door, Greg, the boyfriend, stumbled out of the next trailer into the daylight. He was huge. He looked just as much like an ogre as he sounded, with such a hulking stature that he had to basically squeeze out of the trailer door. He had a full beard, which made his already gigantic head look even bigger, and a big beer belly filled out his faded Grateful Dead T-shirt. He looked right through me and bellowed, "PAZ, where are my goddamn glasses?!" as he approached the old man's motor home. I was still frozen in the doorway, inadvertently blocking his way in. He stopped and directed his question at me to translate. "Ask her what she did with my glasses," he ordered angrily, fixing me fiercely with his eyes. Paz came up behind me. When I told her what he was looking for she said she had no idea. "She hasn't seen them," I said. I noticed that Andrés, having heard the ruckus, had gotten out of the car and was watching. Paz and I both squeezed out of the trailer past Greg, instinctively not wanting to be trapped in the small space with him closing in.

"I know she took my glasses!" he yelled, and then in a drawn-out hiss he said, "I don't trust her." Andrés was still standing there, not moving or understanding the conversation, just watching but alert. I repeated again, this time raising my voice a little, "She said she didn't take your glasses." At that point, Greg made a loud growling sound and lurched at me. But it was a false charge; he stopped short of advancing all the way, pointing his big head at us and growling. For a few seconds, Andrés remained completely poised and frozen, and then his mom started whimpering. Andrés immediately lunged and attacked Greg.

Paz and I staggered backward. The situation was horrifying, not just because of Andrés's sudden uncontrollable rage, but also because he looked so small relative to Greg's hulking mass. Andrés was an average-sized guy by local standards, but up against Greg he looked like a child. But Andrés's rage took Greg completely off guard. Andrés leapt up and grabbed Greg's huge skull in his arms and then, throwing him off balance, slammed

Greg's head into the side of the trailer. Greg's body doubled over, and Andrés started kicking him as he fell to the ground. He kept kicking him as he lay there. Meanwhile, I led Paz, who was now wailing, to the car.

Andrés followed close behind, leaving Greg coughing and sputtering, sprawled on the ground. We drove away, Andrés stone-faced, Paz still crying, and Linda, who had come out of her trailer by then, yelling after us and waving her bone-thin arms in the air, "I'm sorry! I'm so sorry!"

At the source of all the public debate about drugs and all the violence that has resulted from their illegal trade, there lies a single goal: stopping the consumption of drugs. This goal has motivated decades of American "drug wars." Therefore the primary law enforcement strategy implemented in the past few decades has been to cut off the supply of drugs to the United States. Discouraging those who consume drugs by penalizing them is the secondary aim of this top-down strategy of enforcement.

In the United States, decades of narcotics prohibition have helped produce the highest incarceration rate in the world, as well as the highest number of drug users in history. The United States is now the world's largest consumer of every illicit drug on the market. There is a direct relationship between U.S. prohibition policies and recreational drug use and the murder and chaos that have been pushed over the border and unleashed throughout Mexico. In 2009 more people in the United States were consuming illegal drugs than ever before. This was also the same year that in Mexico more people were getting murdered than any year prior. This violence in Mexico has been consistently asymmetrical to that of the United States. For example, in 2010 there were 3,011 murders in Juárez, while directly across the border in El Paso, Texas, there was a total of five (Gibler 2011: 186).

Greg and Linda, American citizens who were pushed for their own reasons across the border, provided just a glimpse of the effects of drug addiction in the United States. This chapter focuses on that other disregarded sphere of the war on drugs: the effects of drug addiction in rural Mexico. I did not formally focus on addiction in my research. I never systematically interviewed addicts. But the experience of family members with loved ones with addictions was a topic that came up regularly in my interviews and informal conversations. There are a number of reasons for considering drug addiction in a book about the cultural and material effects of the war on drugs on the rural poor in Mexico's north. First, drug addiction lies at the heart of the contradictory logic that underpins prohibition efforts: it's the official rationale behind illegality, and, as I will argue, it's also a result of prohibition.

Second, local representations of the trade downplay Mexican consumption and addiction and emphasize that the demand for illegal narcotics is in the United States. If anything, narco-culture celebrates the consumption of *legal* drugs. Corridos and telenovelas include frequent references to the signature whiskey of narcotraffickers, Buchannan's, and often represent narcos drinking and smoking cigarettes. Therefore, the celebration of drug culture in most cultural forms that chronicle the trade valorizes trafficking rather than consumption.

The local view of the United States rather than Mexico as the consumer of drugs sheds light on why the role of the narcotraficante is seen as subversive. It is precisely because the majority of the drugs consumed in the United States are smuggled through northern Mexico that this region is the main battleground for the U.S. war on drugs. The irony is that it is the U.S. prohibition of drugs rather than the Mexican supply of drugs that creates economic opportunities for traffickers. This is part of what makes the role of the narcotraficante a paradoxical site for confrontation with U.S. dominance.

This chapter is based on my observations of the effects of drug addiction on families in the area, effects that were pervasive. I focus on one person from whom I learned the most about the nature and toll of drug addiction on families and relationships. Specifically, I base this chapter principally on what I learned through my friendship with Cruz and my attempts over the years to maintain this friendship through the cycles of his addiction.

THE GHOSTS OF THOSE
YOU USED TO KNOW

Methamphetamine is the drug that has had the most visible effect on the local population. This can be accounted for in part by the recent surge in the drug's availability and affordability.[1]

The production of methamphetamine has been pushed over the border into Mexico over the past decade as a result of increased restrictions and controls on the purchase of some of the crucial ingredients. Mexican methamphetamine production has been increasing dramatically in the past few years since the U.S. government "cracked down" on domestic production in 2005 and introduced regulations that restricted the availability of the chemicals necessary for production.[2] In 2006 U.S. authorities estimated that 80 percent of the methamphetamine on U.S. streets was controlled by Mexican drug traffickers, with most of the supply smuggled in from Mexico.

The drug can be snorted, smoked, or injected. Most people I knew smoked it in a lightbulb through a straw or off of a folded piece of tinfoil. It instantaneously induces feelings of euphoria, exhilaration, and a sharpening of focus. According to the American Psychiatric Association ([1994] 2000), users often become fixated on carrying out repetitive tasks such as cleaning, handwashing, or assembling and disassembling objects. These were the symptoms that were so prominent in Cruz when I first moved into his home in 2005, although at the time he was still a very functional and well-loved member of his family and community.

In 2009 it had been almost three years since I had seen Cruz. By all accounts his drug addiction had become much more disabling, although it was hard to get specific news on Cruz from afar because most of our mutual friends had cut off contact with Cruz. Paz, who was his comadre, had not seen him in years and stopped checking up on him after a series of incidents in which Cruz manipulated her out of money and, on one occasion, siphoned gas from Andrés's truck when she was busy preparing Cruz a snack. She said she didn't trust him anymore. Cruz's children, Javier, Ruby, and Berenice, didn't have much to do with him anymore either. For a time, they stayed with him in the house after their mother, Ana, left him. But Ruby had said that it was impossible to live with Cruz as he started using more and more frequently. At first, random little things started to disappear from the house: Ruby's good mixing bowl, the flat iron for making tortillas. For a while, Ruby would pull the TV set into the sleeping area at night so that Cruz couldn't make off with it. But eventually he managed to sell off all the family's possessions: the refrigerator, even the stove. So his children moved out.

Ruby said he had now sold off everything around him. His living space had shrunk to the 10-by-12-foot room in which they slept. All they had left was their clothing, photographs, and the mattress. He had even sold a small section of the land to his neighbor to park his car for $300. It seemed everything had spiraled into chaos fairly quickly for Cruz. Ruby recounted all this matter-of-factly. I wondered how she could seem so unaffected. Her description evoked a vivid image of Cruz's world closing in around him as he sold off his things and spaces and pushed away his friends and family.

It was sad to imagine Cruz this way, and I wanted to see him. So I went to visit him with Ruby. He had been begging her for grocery money, but she had been putting it off, knowing that he really wanted money for drugs. We stopped at Doña María's, which was the house in the small village Cruz lived in, where one could buy basic supplies (mostly cigarettes and junk food). We grabbed a few bags of instant soups, chips, and a stack of tortillas to bring to Cruz. When we got to his house it was dark. Apparently, Cruz and his girlfriend of the past few years, Pilar (also a meth addict), had lapsed on the electricity payments and had become accustomed to maneuvering by candlelight at night. Since the living space had now been reduced to the bedroom, it apparently wasn't much of a problem.

Ruby yelled for him as we stood outside, but there was no answer. She banged a few times and yelled again. Finally, a frail figure emerged, limping, from around the back. Cruz was hunched over, looking weak and brittle. "What's this?" he asked, annoyed, and grabbed the bag. At first, I thought he hadn't even recognized me, but it turned out that he was simply distracted by the bag—irritated that Ruby had brought food instead of money. They argued for a few moments before he huffed off around back. We left the bag of food beside the front door and then went on our way.

I felt rattled by this encounter. Cruz was so changed, and he had barely acknowledged my presence. During the first phases of my research he had been what anthropologists call a key informant: a person who is especially useful as a source of information and is repeatedly consulted and interviewed in the research process. Cruz quite naturally fell into this role because of his proximity (we lived in the same house) but also because he was charismatic and extremely articulate and loved to talk. As a result, Cruz had a powerful influence on my research as well as my experience living in the region.

I also grew very attached to Cruz personally. During the time that I lived with his family, he would often refer to me as his "youngest daughter." I was actually several years older than even his eldest child, but he said I was the youngest because I was the newest (I also suspected that the designation might have something to do with my initial naïveté). In many ways, I had felt that Cruz was my guide during those years.

But I wasn't always so fond of Cruz. When I first moved in with his family, he terrified me. The first few weeks in his company, I found his mannerisms incredibly disconcerting. As a result of a case of strabismus (a condition that results in crossed eyes) it was difficult to know when he was speaking to me, which was compounded by the fact that he often spoke at a remarkable, drug-induced, speed. But over time I came to admire him greatly. And in the course of our friendship I had witnessed him struggle with, and often overcome, tremendous physical and psychological hardships: a divorce, a bout of full-fledged amnesia, the death of his mother, and chronic suffering from advanced, untreated diabetes.

Cruz dropped out of school when he was eleven years old so he could work for his family. He herded goats full-time for the next five years and also made money by catching rattlesnakes that he would sell to Chinese apothecaries in Mexicali. Over the course of his life he had worked as a fisherman, as a farmhand, selling potable water out of a truck to local villages, and even as a police officer for a short stint before he was fired for, according to him, refusing to take bribes for his bosses.

At the time I met Cruz in 2005, he was collecting and selling scrap metal. Every morning he would climb into the back of a pickup full of several other men from the village and spend all day scavenging and selling scraps of metal they would find in dumps and behind people's houses. But one night, while sweeping the sand in front of his house, he scraped his leg on a thorny bush. His calf and foot swelled up to almost twice their normal size, until he could no longer walk. By the time we got him to the hospital in Mexicali the infection had spread, complicated by his diabetes. The doctors were just barely able to save the leg, but the nerve damage resulted in a permanent limp. With his dragging foot, he couldn't work as easily as he had before.

After my disheartening reunion with Cruz that night with Ruby, I stayed at Ruby's house for a few days. I tried to talk to Cruz again when I saw him walking down the road several days later. I ran up to him and followed him to Doña María's, where he was heading to buy cigarettes. I tried to make small talk and asked after Pilar, his girlfriend. He was not in a good state. He was fidgety and irritated and made this clear in his responses to my questions. "I'll tell you how she is, just fine. Just fine smoking like a fucking chimney. Can't leave your cigarettes around that woman. She just smokes them up one after another, doesn't even pause to breathe between smokes." He was twitching and getting more and more riled up as he talked about Pilar. Then he stopped in his tracks as we turned the corner. Doña María's front door was shut, and the lights in the front were off. It was after 8 P.M., and she had closed shop. Cruz let out a long frustrated sigh and then turned on his heels and headed over to Chucho's house, which was kitty-corner from Doña María's. I knew not to follow him.

I headed back, defeated, to his daughter Ruby's house, still processing the failure of my second attempt to reconnect with Cruz. Javier was there visiting from San Felipe and asked me what was wrong when I walked in. I told him that I had seen Cruz. "We used to be such good friends," I said, "but now it's like..." I hesitated, and Javier completed my sentence for me: "It's like he's not even there anymore." He said this without any drama in his voice, just stating a fact. I realized then that the indifference I had perceived from Cruz's children and Paz was a result of their having already understood that Cruz was no longer himself. He was a ghost that reminded you of the father, compadre, or friend that you once had a long time ago.

Cruz was not an isolated case of addiction among the people I came to know. While drugs may proliferate in the villages in this area because they are for the large part passing through, they don't pass through without leaving a trace. Drug addiction had touched every family I knew in some way. One of the most harrowing indications of drug addiction was the handful of children who regularly got passed around when their drug-addicted mothers were high *(andando cristalinas)*. Neto, eight years old, was the child I got to know best. His mother was a distant cousin of Paz. He lived outside of Santa Ana but would often show up in the village with no one in particular to take care of him for days on end.

Elsa would usually take care of Neto for these stretches of time. She would always express outrage at how dirty he was. Neto showed dramatic signs of neglect: his hair was matted, and his teeth were in terrible shape, not only crooked and protrusive but also visibly rotten. Elsa would scrub him down and instruct him again on how to brush his teeth. But sometimes he would get passed on from Elsa to the neighbor and then back to me if Elsa was working. During the times that I was staying with Paz, I found myself in Neto's company on numerous occasions with no one to pass him off to. Once he came with me for an entire day of interviews in nearby villages because there was nothing else to do with him.

Although his distant relatives in Santa Ana took care of him, they shunned his mother. Elsa would rant passionately about how awful the woman must be to leave the boy like that. Women with addictions experience a strong stigma that is not equally projected onto male drug users. This is usually linked to the expectation that women have more child-rearing responsibilities than men.

Ileana, a twenty-six-year-old woman who was married and had an eight-year-old daughter was a clear example of this double standard. Ileana was already in rough shape by the time I met her in 2005. She was a "picker," which is one of the stereotyped effects of meth on longtime users, because the drug commonly creates the sensation that bugs are crawling all over or under one's skin. Ileana's arms and face often had sores on them from picking at these "imaginary" bugs. Both Ileana and her husband were known to be regular users of cristal, but it was Ileana who experienced the social sanctions of their shared addiction. Many people, both men and women, deliberately ostracized her, often citing her addiction when she had a child she was supposed to care for. Her husband was never subject to these criticisms.

The differences in how drug addiction is understood for men and women in rural Mexico maps onto the similar discrepancy in meaning for men and women involved in the drug trade that I discussed in chapter 1. While drug use does not raise prestige in either case, the stigma is increased for women because of the disproportionate emphasis on their responsibility as mothers in relation to the expectations for fathers.

"DON'T WASTE ANY CIGARETTES ON MY GRAVE"

Cruz weighed on my mind after those encounters I had with him in 2009. A year later when I returned to the area I tried to visit him again, hoping to have better luck. I went up to the front of his house and yelled, "Cruz!!" There was no response, so I yelled again, "Cruz!!!" Silence. I decided I wasn't going to go up to the door and knock. I knew that if he hadn't come out he was either passed out or in a very unpleasant state, and I didn't want to see him if it was either of those options. I was just about to leave when he bounded up behind me and yelled, "Here!!" I was so startled that I let out a little scream, and he laughed maniacally. I started laughing too, relieved. "I knew you were coming," he said excitedly. "Come in, share this caguama with me."

With the bottle of beer tucked under his arm, he led me to the back of the house, since the front door was still boarded up. We crawled over the garbage and the rusted bed frame behind the house to get inside, where his girlfriend was. I kissed her hello as Cruz kept talking. He said he knew I was coming because he had had a dream that I came. "I told Pilar, 'My youngest is coming back to Mexico. I saw it in a dream.' Isn't that right, Pilar? I told you, didn't I?" She nodded, unimpressed. His dreams predict things. This is something he'd talked about on many previous occasions. "Just the other day I dreamed a man stopped by from Mexicali. A friend who was passing through. And he came the very next day."

Cruz kept talking, detailing the familiar litany of premonitions he has had over his lifetime. As he talked, I looked around the room. It was the first time I had been in the house since I had lived there almost four years before. It was the first time I had witnessed its shrinkage myself. It had never been a luxurious house. In fact, like most in the village, it would be better characterized as a shack. It never had things like running water or glass or screens in the windows. Nonetheless, at one point Cruz had taken a lot of pride in this home. He had built it himself, and as he would regularly point out, it was the first in the village to have concrete floors. All the other houses had had dirt floors at the time. When I lived there with his family, it also had some functional living spaces, including a living area with a couch and a TV and a kitchen.

But now it was just this one room. One wall was patched together with plywood and Styrofoam, and the other three left standing were made of cinderblock. There were large cracks splitting the concrete floor, no doubt from the earthquake that had taken place in April 2010. The magnitude was 7.2 on the Richter scale (the earthquake in Haiti that same year was 7.0), but the epicenter was in such a remote region that there was little media coverage and only one death.

The window was boarded up. One wall was covered with photographs of his family; the other wall, with centerfolds of naked women from porn magazines. I looked at all the photos of his family. I had taken many of them myself and noticed that they were no longer in the frames in which I had given them to him. He had most likely sold those along with everything else. Pilar was sitting on the mattress between the two walls of images, smoking cigarettes. We sat and shared the caguama as the little room filled with smoke and Cruz kept talking.

I was so happy to be in his company again and to feel welcome there that I tried not to dwell on the obvious signs that he was extraordinarily high. He was rambling on at full speed, and the conversation was all over the place. Suddenly he was talking about my eyebrows: "Remember when Manuela [the neighbor] tried to get you to pluck out your eyebrows?" he laughed. "Well, Pilar naturally has none at all," he said. "She has to draw them on." Pilar nodded from the bed, smoking her cigarette. "She paints them on every day," he added, as she nodded again. Then Cruz went on to tell a story about how once his niece came to the door and knocked when Pilar had just woken up. Pilar went to the door and opened it, and when the niece looked at her face she erupted in the most terrified scream you had ever heard. She just stood there looking at Pilar and screaming. Pilar's drawn-on eyebrows had gotten all smudged as she slept, he explained, and they were twisted up into a fierce-looking frown. We all laughed at the image of Pilar standing there, confused by his niece's screams with a hideous frown smudged on her forehead.

But I couldn't help but note that Cruz and Pilar, who were both attractive people not long ago, looked rather frightening in general these days. Messy fake eyebrows aside, Pilar was gaunt and bug-eyed. Cruz was even skinnier than the last time I had seen him. This was highlighted by the fact that on the wall beside me there was a photo of Cruz from five years ago—a glaring reminder of how much he had changed. In the photo, Cruz, Ana (his former wife), and I are sitting on a bench in a shopping mall in Mexicali. We are all eating ice cream cones and look caught off guard by the photo. Cruz was a big guy then, broad in the shoulders and with a fuller face, and in the photo his big belly is prominently displayed.

I tried to change the subject, asking about el Día de los Muertos (the Day of the Dead), which was a few days before. I asked if

Cruz had gone to the cemetery. He said he had not gone and started complaining about the ritual: "People here are obsessed with death. You know what they do here, right? In Mexico, for the Day of the Dead people go to the cemetery and take gifts of food and chocolate and cigarettes, and they just throw it in there to leave on their graves. My sister goes and takes my mom's favorite food—just leaves it there for her. That's right, now that she's dead! She came by here to take me with her, but I told her I didn't want to go." I asked, "You don't believe that your spirit stays around when you die?" He shook his head. "No," he said. "I believe that when you die you're dead. I also told her I don't want her wasting any food or cigarettes on my grave when I'm dead. I said to her, 'Why not bring it to me now, when I'm alive?'" He laughed. "'Go ahead. Whatever you were planning to bring me then, just give it to me now when I can actually use it!'" We all laughed at this, and Cruz continued, "What I don't like about the people around here is that they wait to take care of you like that—until after you die. They wait to go to the graves and pray."

"ALL THAT I HARVEST, I SEND TO THE GRINGOS"

My impression was that Cruz's comments about people caring for the dead instead of the living had as much to do with his own feelings of abandonment as it did with his observations about the ritual itself. Cruz, who was from a mestizo fishing community, was critical of both Mexican and indigenous influences on his community. He also had a particularly incisive critique of the U.S. influence on the region.

While Cruz was uncomfortable talking about his own addiction, he had been very articulate over the years I had known him about the effect of the drug trade on the area and the political scenario by which Mexico had become the largest supplier of drugs to the United States. Ironically, Cruz was particularly eloquent about U.S. responsibility for the success of Mexico's drug economy. "All the drugs that come from these places, from Colombia and Mexico, where are they going? Who is the biggest consumer of drugs? The United States. The drugs that these countries are producing aren't for their personal use. They're for the biggest consumer in the world: the United States." Cruz described an occasion when he had gotten into a heated argument with a gringo about Mexican drug smuggling and about the U.S. scorn directed at the trade and its associated violence in Mexico. "I said to the American, 'And who consumes these drugs? Your people.'"

Cruz had never been forthcoming about his own addiction. Whenever the subject came up he would simply repeat that he could stop using at any time. He only spoke about it in very general terms. But to his family and neighbors his habits were obvious. Everyone knew when Cruz went off to get high. He would head over to Chucho's, or Yoli's, or Chico's, a few of the half dozen houses in the village where he was sure to be able to score. There were a handful of reliable backup sources nearby in Santa Ana and Sauzalito that he would resort to when he owed money to all the dealers in his own village. He never had to go all the way to the city.

Cruz's insistence that the consumption of drugs in the United States, not Mexico, was the source of the problem for both countries—while appearing hypocritical in the context of his situation—fell in line with wider discourses among locals and smugglers in the area. For example, as mentioned earlier, while corridos glorify the trafficking of drugs, they rarely celebrate illegal consumption. Instead, they stress the role of the United

States in the drug trade, often pointing out that the United States is the destination of the majority of drugs produced and shipped from Latin America.

Scholars of corridos argue that the idea that drugs are sold and consumed exclusively in the United States is propagated in the lyrics of many corridos (see, e.g., Villalobos and Ramírez-Pimenta 2004). In one popular song by Los Tucanes de Tijuana, the protagonist sings that he will continue working as long as there is demand in the United States: "Where the best customers are, they buy one hundred kilos of dust as if they were buying flowers."[3] There are many corridos that express similar attitudes. Another song by Los Tucanes states, "All that I harvest, I send to the gringos."

Yet the huge demand in the United States and, in particular, the circulation of drugs through northern Mexico has also meant that some drugs have become extremely accessible and relatively affordable in the region. This is especially true of methamphetamine because it is manufactured there, not just transported through. As we shall see, one of the reasons that this area has seen a stark rise in addiction rates in rural colonias is precisely because drugs are illegal and thus both a valuable and an unregulated commodity.

HOW TO COUNT YOUR WAY THROUGH AN EARTHQUAKE

A few weeks after my visit to Cruz's house, I was driving down Route 5 to visit some fishing camps in the gulf. The road cuts through stark and vacant desert, which stretches out in white sand and salt flats under the blue sky. For miles and miles there is no sign of any other human presence, just the desert and the two-lane highway. I came upon a long stretch of abandoned construction where the road had been dug up. This stretch of highway had been undergoing construction for years, and I had read in the paper that the project had been on hiatus. So there were several hundred meters of dug-up, unpaved road. I drove slowly, sending up a cloud of sand and dust—grateful that it was at least broad daylight.

When I drove out of the cloud and onto the place the paved road began, I saw the construction crew's equipment parked on the shoulder: a steamroller, an excavator, and a bulldozer. There was also a solitary figure sitting on the seat of the bulldozer. It looked just like Cruz sitting there, as if on a throne, surveying the scene. I slowed to a stop, thinking that perhaps I was imagining things. But when I looked up again he was walking over. He looked angry. "Have you seen Pilar?" he asked frantically. "No," I said, and before I could ask why he spit out a series of obscenities, saying he had been waiting there on the road, in the middle of nowhere, since the day before. "I ran out of cigarettes yesterday, and she was supposed to bring me … food." He was trembling. "You've been here since yesterday? What are you doing here? What happened?" I asked, confused. He looked irritated by my questions, muttering as if it was utterly beside the point, "They're paying me to guard the equipment."

I offered him a ride, but he said he couldn't leave the equipment and had to wait for Pilar. I was inclined to ask a dozen more questions, but I couldn't stand being around him in this state and wanted to drive away. I quickly rifled through the stuff in the back of the car and gave him water and a bag of oranges. He didn't look hungry. He eyed the pack of cigarettes on the dash. I grabbed it and joked, "Here. I was going to wait until you were dead to give you these, but I guess you can have them now." I couldn't help but want to refer to earlier conversations when he was like this, trying to get some kind of confirmation that he was the same person and that he remembered me from just several weeks before. He didn't even smile but grabbed the pack and said, "Thanks."

I drove away unsettled, overcome with the uncanny sense this kind of encounter with Cruz inspired. When the cloud of dust from the construction site disappeared behind the horizon in my rearview mirror, I wondered again if I had imagined the whole scene. As I approached San Felipe and finally got a signal on my cell, I called Cruz's daughter—partly because I felt guilty leaving him there and partly because I wanted to verify his story. Ruby explained in a familiar tone of detached exasperation that he had been working there for two weeks, guarding the construction equipment. He got the job through a friend who worked on the crew. "They are paying him a lot to just sit there all day. He spends it all on meth for himself and Pilar, and he hasn't saved a cent. Pilar has to bring him everything, and she has to get rides to do it," Ruby said. "But sometimes she forgets."

Two days later, I drove back up the same road, hoping that he wouldn't still be there. But there he was, up on the landing, pacing around the equipment. He was wearing different clothes and seemed to have a sloppy red turban fastened to his head (a T-shirt on closer inspection—presumably to protect from the sun and wind). When he saw my car he gave me a huge smile and a salute. Pilar had apparently made a visit. As soon as I stepped out of the vehicle, he launched into a description of everything that had happened in the previous few days as he ascended his throne on the bulldozer. I climbed up on the excavator beside him and sat as he continued to describe in impeccable detail everything that passed by in the last two days.

He explained in more detail what he was doing there, which he had been too agitated to do a few days before. He said he first got the job to watch the vehicles and equipment just at night when the workers went home. So, at first, he would stay there all night and hitchhike the hour or so up the road home in the daytime. But since the construction stopped, he had to stay there all day too. He said it was pretty bad out there, boring and lonely, but the pay was amazing. He received US$200 a week just to be there all the time.

As a nearly imperceptible tremor shivered through the equipment, we froze for a second. It was another aftershock. There had been several already that day, as there had been most days since the big one in April, several months before. Cruz asked if I felt the earthquake the previous night. I had been awakened by it but fell asleep pretty quickly. Cruz told me the aftershock the night before had lasted twenty-eight seconds.

The first time I experienced an earthquake was under his roof years before. It was a moderate one, 5.5 on the Richter scale. I was shocked by the sensation of the world rattling and instinctively ran from the house. On the street, the swaying electrical poles confirmed that it was not just the house shaking. Cruz had laughed uproariously and proceeded to lecture me on the nature of earthquakes. It was a lecture that I would hear variations of many times thereafter: "The first thing people do when they feel a tremor is they run out of their houses. But that's the worst thing you can do!" Cruz stood up on the broad seat of the bulldozer, excited to be on one of his favorite topics. "Most of the people that get hurt in an earthquake get hurt when they're trying to run out of their house," he said. "That's why I count." He lifted his finger in the air to emphasize this point.

His eyes were shining brightly now. "If you count the seconds as they pass you stay in control."

"How many seconds did the big one in April last?" I asked. "Did you count that one?" Cruz nodded his head and said that it lasted 88 seconds. He explained that he was driving through Sauzalito when it started. "I started counting as soon as the tremors began and immediately pulled the car over. It was mayhem on the street. At 15 seconds, the ground split open and water started shooting out. At 26 seconds, people started dropping to their knees and praying up to the heavens." Cruz dropped to the floor to imitate the people on the street, clasping his hands together in prayer. "Did you drop to your knees too, Cruz?" I asked, misunderstanding his imitation. "Hell no! I just kept counting. At 88 seconds, the ground stopped shaking. And then silence! That's the longest earthquake I've ever counted!" he exclaimed.

I watched Cruz hold forth against the backdrop of that beautiful day. The desert stretched out in all directions in soothing, sandy, monochromatic tones against his dark skin and deep red turban. I stood up on my seat too as Cruz kept talking to see what it all looked like from his perspective. I felt a rush of adrenaline as his words tumbled over me: calculations about earthquakes and tremors and raging intimations of his momentary megalomania. I stayed there for several hours, lingering until the very last of the sun set over the shimmering horizon. I hesitated to leave, as I knew things would probably be different the next time I saw him.

PROHIBITION AND THE INCREASED ACCESSIBILITY OF DRUGS

According to official discourses in the United States and Mexico, the reason that drugs are illegal is because they damage communities. They are illegal because of the suffering experienced by people like Cruz and Greg and Linda, the American meth addicts in the campo. The logic is that prohibiting the sale of drugs, in addition to sending a moral message, should make them less accessible. As the violence associated with drug trafficking and addiction continues to worsen, the rationale for prohibition policies is sustained. The strategy reproduces its own justification: by fueling a continual crisis of addiction, crime, and other drug-related problems, prohibition policies necessitate further investment in the enforcement purportedly required to address these problems (Bertram et al. 1996: 177).

Aspects of this circular logic are clearly unraveling under the atrocities of current conditions. Certainly the tens of thousands of gruesome deaths and disappearances in the past six years of the war on drugs are far worse for communities than even the most horrendous effects of rampant meth addiction. But here I want to highlight the less obvious hypocrisy of prohibition: the mistaken assumption that drugs will be less available if they are illegal. This is particularly clear in Cruz's experiences. In places like Santa Ana, Sauzalito, and Cruz's village, much like many of the rural villages in the borderlands, drugs have become more available as prohibition efforts have escalated. The flow of drugs through the area and the local production of drugs have also fueled higher rates of addiction among the rural poor. By 2008, 51 percent more people in Mexico were addicted to drugs than just six years earlier.[4] While the number of methamphetamine labs seized by Mexican authorities has increased significantly in the past five years, shipments across the border have continued to grow. According to the U.S. National Drug Intelligence Center, "Law enforcement and intelligence reporting, as well as seizure, price, and purity data, indicate that the availability of methamphetamine in general is increasing in markets in every region of the country."[5]

Philippe Bourgois (2003) observed this dynamic firsthand in his research on inner-city Harlem. He points out that, ironically, decriminalization would make drugs less accessible to youths in the inner city because it would no longer be worthwhile for dealers to hawk their wares in small quantities on street corners. A similar irony is evident in the levels of potency of the drugs available in the United States. A former drug prosecutor I met named James E. Gierach, who now speaks publicly on the failures of prohibition policies, told me in an interview that when he started as a drug prosecutor in the early 1970s the highest-quality heroin available on the streets of Chicago was at an average purity level of 2 percent. Now, after more than forty years of prohibition and police crackdowns, the purity of heroin is 90 percent.[6]

Therefore, nationwide trends in both the United States and Mexico indicate that prohibition has not had the effect of making drugs less available. Instead, prohibition has fueled the expansion of criminal networks and facilities such that there has never been greater availability of highly potent drugs in the United States or Mexico. These national statistics come to life when watching someone like Cruz in his everyday consumer patterns. For example, when Doña María's shop closes for the night back in the village, he's out of all reliable options to buy cigarettes but still has a slew of options available to him to purchase meth. Consider the day I saw him on the road rushing to Doña María's store to replace the cigarettes Pilar had smoked. When he found the store was closed he huffed right across the street to Chucho's to buy meth.

While drugs are more easily accessible than ever before, treatment options for addicts are scarce. Early on in my fieldwork when I was living in Cruz's house (in 2005 and 2006), I took part in discussions with his family about drug rehabilitation. At first the conversations focused on the difficulty of finding a center; most of them were far away, in Tijuana and Mexicali. We also discussed the high cost of treatment and the difficulty of being able to convince Cruz to go.

In more recent years, all talk of detox centers has become irrelevant. As narcotics addiction increases in Mexico, drug rehabilitation centers have become battlegrounds in the country's escalating drug war violence. Hired guns from cartels often use rehab clinics as hideouts after committing high-profile assassinations, making the centers targets for revenge by their rivals. Almost every month there are reports of armed squads breaking into rehab centers and gunning down those thought to be rivals from competing narcotics syndicates, along with all the other patients who happen to be there too. In the past several years, there have been dozens of attacks on rehab centers in border cities.[7] In this context, discussions with Cruz's family about getting him into a rehab clinic have ceased entirely.

Unfortunately, both the United States and Mexico approach consumption and addiction by taking punitive measures. In the past several decades incarceration rates have skyrocketed in the United States.[8] Large numbers of users are locked up on possession charges, only to find that drugs are easily available in prison (Andreas 2009). It is for all these reasons that many critics have argued for the urgency of a different approach to the drug problem that would treat drug addiction as a public health problem rather than a security issue. A widely cited 1994 study by the RAND Corporation, a well-known conservative think tank, concluded that $34 million invested in treatment reduces cocaine use as much as $366 million invested in interdiction.[9]

However, until there is such a restructuring of the priorities of government investment in the problem of drug addiction, people like Cruz have very few options and no support for recovering from their addictions. Furthermore, the people closest to Cruz have no recourse for helping him and few options for even keeping him in their lives. The nature of Cruz's escalating addiction meant that it was impossible to predict when he would be on the up or the down. It made it impossible to navigate a relationship with him. It also made it impossible to know if he was speaking the truth or to trust any of his actions. Months after the day we talked for hours while surveying the world from the vantage point of his throne, I looked up information about the big earthquake that April that Cruz described. I wondered how accurate his counting was or if he was in fact just making it all up. The record states that the earthquake lasted 89 seconds. His count was only one second off.

FIVE

Moving the Money When the Bank Accounts Get Full

It did not occur to me that Don Emmanuel was professionally involved in anything other than the purchase and sale of fish until long after I met him. Over the years I had crossed paths with him often, especially during the fishing seasons. Because I had a long-standing research interest in water scarcity and local fishing conflicts, I would run into him in many of the small fishing villages in the region. I would come through to visit and do interviews. He would come through to visit and arrange purchases. He would hire locals in each of the villages to pack his trucks, and he also worked hard to maintain good relationships with the fishing crews and their families. But for the most part I tried to stay out of Don Emmanuel's way, largely because his religious zealotry made me uncomfortable.

By 2010 I could no longer avoid Don Emmanuel because he had taken an increasing interest in my friend Isabella, Andrés's former girlfriend. Isabella's life had fallen into disarray after her son was born. She had a drinking problem and was prone to aggressive outbursts. When her son, Chepe, was two years old she went to jail for a short period for aggravated assault. During a drunken brawl, she had threatened to kill another woman and broken a beer bottle over her head. But after serving her sentence I had heard she was doing much better. I went to her house a few months later to see Isabella and her family but learned from her mother that she had gone into town with Don Emmanuel to go to church. This was intriguing, as it was completely out of character for Isabella.

When they arrived home, finally, Isabella extolled the virtues of the experience, exclaiming, "I had no idea it would be so beautiful!" She went on to say that the liturgy was really interesting as well. Her attitude toward Don Emmanuel was so obsequious and she was so transparent in the way she was ingratiating herself with him that I was even more intrigued by their strengthened friendship.

We went outside and sat on the front stoop so Isabella could smoke a cigarette and fill me in on what had been going on. Chepe followed us and stayed close by, ambling noisily back and forth on his little tricycle. Isabella didn't like it when Chepe got close enough to inhale her secondhand smoke, so she told him to do some circles on his trike to keep him busy and out of reach of the smoke. "Give me six," she said. Chepe started some circles. "Those are baby circles," she corrected, realizing he would be done in no time. "Do some big kid circles." So Chepe pedaled farther away, circling long and wide enough for her to finish her cigarette.

Meanwhile, Isabella told me that Don Emmanuel had taken her on as a kind of moral project, counseling her, teaching her how to be a better person, and showing her the "right path." She didn't really buy into any of the religious part, she said, but she liked him and thought he was a good guy. She also mentioned that he was trying to do good things for the community. "Besides," she smiled, with what I noticed was a more characteristic flash of mischief in her eye, "he's clearly rich."

Don Emmanuel was also close with Paz's family. He bought fish from Elsa and Rafa's fishing crew and for several years had fronted them money for various pieces of equipment they had needed to purchase before the fishing season. On a few occasions, we had meals together with Paz's family. He seemed completely out of place in Paz's humble little house with his nicely pressed and collared shirt, leather loafers, and dark blue jeans. He ate with a knife and fork and rolled up his tortillas, eating them on the side, instead of breaking off pieces and eating his food with them like everyone else. Then he would wipe his mouth meticulously with a paper napkin. His formality was in sharp contrast to the screaming babies and the kids climbing around and the flies intermittently landing here and there. His presence was plainly unnerving.

But Paz's family and the other fishing families in the region always treated Don Emmanuel with respect. Paz and her mother doted on him by attending to his every need and cooking for him. Everyone called him "Don," an honorific used in Mexico to indicate status and express respect. He also provoked a huge amount of speculation: about his past as a priest, his family and businesses back in Mexico City, and just how rich he really was. Both Isabella and Elsa had mentioned at various points that he had lots of money. I asked how they knew. "You can tell by his car and his clothes," Isabella said. She said that he runs several businesses and owns the trailers that he uses to transport fish. "But he's cheap. He never pays for anything, he never buys anything: food, beer, nothing." Meanwhile, Don Emmanuel himself was, for the most part, very quiet. He barely interacted with the children, although Elsa told me that he had several adult children of his own. In fact, he didn't seem to talk at all unless he was delivering some kind of lecture. And when he did embark on one of his orations, he managed to command the undivided attention of his audience.

One night, I witnessed the enraptured audience at such a lecture. There were a handful of people on Paz's porch after the fishing crews had returned home and cleaned up. The sun had set, and we all sat around drinking instant coffee. This was when Don Emmanuel gently drew us all into a lesson about God's love. "All love must begin with the love of God," he began. "You can't know true love for a man unless you know the love of God." He continued, "A woman can go from man to man, from one man to the next. But that is no way to live your life. If you go from one relationship to the next and one relationship produces a child, then that is not what is best for the child."

Doña Luisa, Paz's mother, interrupted politely, "Men also go from one relationship to the next." I had interpreted his gender-specific phrasing as an indication that he was, though speaking abstractly, intending this particular sermon for Isabella's personal benefit. Isabella often talked about the travails of being a single mother in Don Emmanuel's presence. Don Emmanuel nodded in agreement with Doña Luisa as if the fact that men also behaved this way was an obvious yet irrelevant piece of information, and then he continued.

"When you have children, you want what is best for the child, right?" He turned to me, looking for confirmation. I said, "I don't have children," smugly, as if, as a result of this fact, he couldn't draw me in to support his argument. "Yes, but if you did . . . ," he pressed. Then he turned to Isabella and said, "And of course, if you have a child when it is not the right moment—without the blessing of God—then your life is derailed. You can't finish school; you can't achieve your career goals. Your life is put on hold." Isabella, nodding her head repentantly, responded, "That's for sure!"

I started to steal glances around the group, trying to ascertain how everyone else was reacting to Don Emmanuel's speech. I watched Elsa's face as she listened. Her attention was completely focused on him. But it was impossible to interpret her expression. The grandmother, on the other hand, was clearly irritated by how gender-specific his lecture was. Twice she jumped in to correct his skewed allegations of the wantonness of women. But she didn't seem to take issue with the way he was appropriating love as an exclusive capacity of true believers. By the end of his speech, he had argued that all our actual and hypothetical children, as well as any "man" that might be at our side, would remain unloved until we found the path of God.

Finally, as it grew late and Paz went inside to start putting the children to bed, Don Emmanuel politely bade us goodnight. When he was gone, Elsa turned to me and in full earshot of Isabella said, sarcastically, "It's so true what Don Emmanuel says. If it weren't for that damn kid, Isabella would surely be a doctor or a lawyer by now." Paz started laughing from inside the house. The tension of the past few hours was suddenly broken. Isabella threw a piece of bread at Elsa. "Perra!" (Bitch), she hissed but then, laughing, continued the fantasy. "If it weren't for this little brat," she cooed as she picked up Chepe, getting ready to head home herself, "Mommy would be driving around in a brand-new car, wearing a power suit, and defending big-shot clients in court!"

Though intended as a dig at Isabella, Elsa's comment was also an implicit critique of a view that both development workers and religious missionaries who frequent the area share. They believe that bad personal decisions are what stand in the way of upward mobility for Mexico's poor. Rather than recognize the wider conditions of political repression and poverty into which many people are born, the idea is that if only kids weren't having premarital sex they would all be successful professionals by now. Similarly, Don Emmanuel's proselytizing emphasized the importance of individual choices: avoid premarital sex, stay away from drugs and alcohol, and learn to save your money instead of spending it immediately. That was, Don Emmanuel argued, how the people of Santa Ana could pull themselves out of poverty.

One theme that was emphasized by Don Emmanuel, as well as the doctors, missionaries, and development workers who came through the villages, was the "mismanagement" of money. As they often commented *"los pobres"* (the poor) spend whatever money they earn right away, never saving up for purchases that might actually improve their overall quality of life (indoor plumbing was the most commonly touted cause for such savings). But the message seemed more effective coming from Don Emmanuel, largely because he was obviously successful. He drove a relatively new Honda Civic, his clothes were always impeccable, and, as many commented in reference to his distant past as a priest, he nonetheless seemed "real." He was down-to-earth and a "good guy."

I realized that Don Emmanuel's preaching on financial management had actual practical implications for some people one day while chatting with Ramón, the son of one of the neighbors. Ramón, like many young people in the area, worked for a low wage cleaning the fish caught on any given tide (usually just a few cents a fish). He was excited because he made a lot of money on the first tide and especially because he was saving it. "I have a bank account now," he said, and he told me he was planning to put some money in the bank the next time he made a trip into the city. "You opened a bank account?" I asked, surprised, for I had heard of very few people from the village keeping money in a bank. "Yes, Don Emmanuel got one for me," he said. And at that point, he took out his bank card and showed it to me, saying, "I'm going to save a lot of money."

Later I asked Elsa if she knew Don Emmanuel was opening bank accounts for people in the village. She nodded. He had opened accounts for her and Isabella too, telling them they needed to start saving up for the future. "I got 2,000 pesos from him for my account" (about US$200), she said in a satisfied tone. Hesitantly, I asked why he would have paid her to do something that he claimed was for her own good. "Because I just laughed at him and told him, 'I wasn't born yesterday,'" she said. She told me that she had known about his money laundering ever since the day he had fronted the money for her and Rafa's crew: boat, truck, and nets, all in U.S. cash.

It was then that I realized why Don Emmanuel had been so insistent about the virtues of saving. The opening of bank accounts clearly served another purpose for him, as a way of laundering money. When drug money arrives in Mexico, this money is, by and large, useless to the cartels. Before it can be used, it must be transferred to legitimate bank accounts and businesses. Officials in Mexico believe the amount of laundered money could be as high as $45 billion a year.[1] For the most part, this flow of money starts in the United States, the world's largest market for illegal drugs, and comes back to drug cartels in Mexico through a variety of illicit routes: electronic transfers, hidden in luggage brought across the border, packed inside the tires or panels of trucks and cars, hidden in airplanes and often on the bodies of mules.

Money launderers typically work under contract for traffickers who hire them for a fee. The launderer's job is to get the funds into the financial system unnoticed and sometimes to physically transport the cash in and out of the country. The first and most sensitive stage is getting the cash into the banking system, and this is also the stage that is most vulnerable to detection. One way to mitigate the risk is to launder funds through small accounts, which are then transferred to other accounts.[2] This is a technique called "smurfing," which appeared to be what Don Emmanuel was doing with Ramón's account, although, as we shall see, he relied on a number of other techniques as well.

THE PHYSICALITY OF FINANCE

For most middle-class North Americans, it has become natural to think of modern finance as increasingly abstract and virtual. Credit card transactions, e-banking, and electronic payments, as well as stock values and equity scores, have removed the majority of financial transactions from the exchange of cash between individuals. Indeed, a growing number of outlets, airlines, for example, won't accept cash for a purchase as small as a bag of pretzels ("credit only"). It's increasingly common for people to go several days without touching a single dollar bill now that electronic transactions are so prevalent.

Social scientists have documented this historical progression. They have affirmed that we live in a time of economic virtualism where financial abstractions remove economic activity from the broader social face-to-face contexts in which it had existed.

James Carrier (2001) argues that abstract neo-economics is in the process of a conscious attempt to make the real world conform to the virtual image, moving to greater abstraction and virtualism. He argues that economic thought is creating a virtual reality by reduction and by disembedding money from engaged, human relationships. In anthropology, this same story of the great transformation of money from socially embedded to abstract has been told: from barter and trade to coin to paper and evolving ultimately to increasing distance from actual things to "derivatives," "shareholder values," and so on (Maurer 2005: 100).

Some scholars have criticized this interpretation, arguing that the idea of money as abstract has become a dominant Western "folk theory." For example, Karen Ho, in *Liquidated: An Ethnography of Wall Street* (2009), argues against dominant representations of investment banks as part of abstract, all-powerful global markets. Instead, she shows that "the market" is actually made up of individuals and groups that engage in face-to-face activities and decision-making processes that are situated and shaped by specific cultural and ideological norms. David Graeber, in *Debt: The First 5,000 Years* (2011), complicates the progressive narrative of modern finance from another angle. He argues that what we know as "money" started off not with the minting of coinage but with "debt" and "credit," which have existed since long before other forms of monetary exchange.

Below I draw from this body of literature to highlight that much of the local economic impact of the traffic of money is, rather than abstract and disembodied, profoundly material. I explore how mules in northern Mexico smuggle thousands of American dollars in cash hidden on their bodies through military checkpoints. Money laundering not only forces us to focus on the material properties of money and the way it is socially embedded but also requires a rethinking of the relationship between the free market and illicit economies.

WHEN THE BANK GETS FULL AND THERE'S TOO MUCH MONEY TO COUNT

After my conversations with Ramón and Elsa, I started to see some of Don Emmanuel's interactions and activities from a different perspective. For example, one day in front of Don Pedro's store, which he ran out the side window of his house in Santa Ana, I heard Don Emmanuel encouraging the Martinez brothers, all in their late teens and early twenties, to be more responsible about "saving their money" (the Martinez brothers were big drinkers, especially after a good tide brought a high yield of fish). I came upon the conversation as he was inquiring about their mother, who had recently recovered from a bad illness. "Thank the Lord for your mother's health," he said as I walked around to Don Pedro's window. "Now, guys," he said, "on the next tide you'll be making a lot of money. Are you ready for the tide?" They nodded in anticipation, mentioning that they had gotten their nets all fixed up. They were already estimating how many tons they could bring in between their families' two crews.

As I walked away from Don Pedro's store with my purchases, Don Emmanuel was taking the conversation to what had now become a familiar strategic crossroads in his logic. "And if your mother becomes ill again, you'll want to be able to take care of her, won't you? You'll want to take care of your family?" I had walked out of earshot by the time the Martinez boys could answer. But one can guess that they would indeed want to take care of their sick mom. Don Emmanuel could argue anyone into agreeing with all the leading points in one of his arguments, and this one was surely leading to that part of "God's path" where one would work hard to save money.

Because I was becoming increasingly curious about how Don Emmanuel's operation worked, I asked Isabella about it. She took out her bank card to confirm Elsa's claim that she had one too. "Do you know how much money he moves through your account?" I asked. She shook her head. "No idea," she said. "Aren't you curious?" I asked. "You know you can see all the transactions if you go to an automatic teller." Isabella just shrugged and replied, "Yeah, but we'd have to get all the way to the city to find one of those machines." It seemed that Isabella and Elsa were not particularly interested in the mechanics of Don Emmanuel's operation. They also seemed removed enough in their daily lives (the banks and bank machines were hours away in the city) to not feel particularly at risk given their mundane involvement.

It is apparent from Elsa's, Isabella's, and Ramón's experiences that Don Emmanuel had a number of strategies to accomplish the initial placement of cash besides the classic "front business" strategy for laundering money. The laundering of funds through small accounts, which are then transferred to other accounts, in this case involved people whose financial identities could be easily manipulated. This operation was developed through a network of people who effectively insulated Don Emmanuel from the risks. He outsourced those tasks to mules and smurfs such as Ramón, who absorb most of the human risks and potential costs. Don Emmanuel relied on the complicity of many of those who, in turn, relied on his resources.

Don Emmanuel's network of smurfs has implications for the classic narrative that in modern finance economic activities become increasingly abstracted from the social contexts and relationships in which they previously took place. This case shows how laundering is accomplished through the cultivation of long-term personal relationships. As time passed, I saw how these relationships and the reciprocities they created facilitated Don Emmanuel's money laundering in a number of cases. For example, on one occasion Elsa's cousin Lupita became very ill when she was with her husband in Mexico City, where he was stationed as a military officer. Because her husband was working, someone had to be sent to bring Lupita and her six-month-old baby back to the village near the border where she could be looked after. None of her family members had the time or the resources to travel to Mexico City and back.

Ultimately it was Don Emmanuel who drove thirty-six hours to bring Lupita to the village. It seemed like a reasonable arrangement because he often traveled to Mexico City on business anyway. But Lupita suggested that now her husband, Antonio, was going to owe Don Emmanuel "a big favor." I remembered that years earlier Lupita had said that Antonio had transferred to Mexico City, in part to extricate himself precisely from these kinds of relationships of reciprocity and obligation, which sometimes complicated his military alliances. It seemed, ironically, that he had not gone far enough by moving to Mexico City.

Months after the fact, Lupita recounted the trip to me. Don Emmanuel picked up a bundle of cash when they passed through Mexico City and had her carry it in every available place, including all pockets and the baby's diaper. They were hundred-dollar bills. She didn't know how much, but "it was a lot." She emphasized that the experience was marked by the bodily discomfort created by the physical presence of the money. It was hot, she was sick, and the baby was uncomfortable and crying. They drove that way all the way from Mexico City to Mexicali. She said they must have passed through about a dozen military checkpoints.

I asked her why he had to take the money to Mexicali. "His accounts in Mexico City were all full," she said. At first this comment just struck me as naive. It seemed to indicate that Lupita did not understand what a bank account was; technically speaking, bank accounts do not get "full." She clearly thought that bank accounts were physical spaces that could "fill up" once enough cash was deposited in them. This would be a natural assumption for Lupita, who had grown up in a rural impoverished community where a huge majority of inhabitants had never set foot in a bank but instead kept their money in shoeboxes, sock drawers, and jars. That is, they kept money in things that indeed "fill up."

In retrospect I realized that Lupita's interpretation was actually quite insightful. Because of anti–money laundering measures, Mexican banks are legally required to report deposits over a certain amount of money. Currently, the limit for deposits is $4,000 a month in an individual's account and $7,000 in a business account.[3] This means that whatever bank accounts Don Emmanuel would have had access to in Mexico City would have effectively become "full" after a limited series of deposits.

Lupita's interpretation of why the money had to be moved from one place to another highlights another important point about the way money laundering is understood by many of those people vulnerable enough to find themselves smuggling cash: the sheer materiality of money. This materiality is most salient for those who work, as Lupita and her baby did, as mules, storing money on their bodies to pass through security checkpoints.

Lupita could not estimate with any accuracy the amount of cash they were carrying. She said there was so much that at more than one rest stop she was tempted to hide a bill away for herself. Her confession made me nervous. I said that just because there was so much money didn't mean he was going to be less likely to count it. But Lupita argued that there were so many bills that it would indeed be harder for Don Emmanuel to keep track, especially because he was spending money on food and gas the whole way. She didn't take any, however; she just experienced the temptation. After all, he was doing her a favor giving them a ride to Mexicali, and Lupita thought that Don Emmanuel was *"muy buena gente"* (a really good person). She said he even bought a car seat for the baby because he said it was safer, a gesture Lupita thought was both excessive and testimony to what a good person he is.

Therefore, the quantitative value of money for Lupita was an expression of the object's material quality: its size and number. This quantity was also how Lupita rationalized that they were moving so much of it in the first place (since the bank accounts were full). By now, it should be more apparent why the idea that money has become "virtual," "deterritorialized," and "disembodied" does not resonate for mules crossing checkpoints with thousands of dollars of cash formed to their bodies. But it is also important to reflect on how this perception of money could inform theorizations of the market generally.

Money laundering activities such as those described here are not just at the fringes of modern economic processes. Nor are they an exotic counterexample of how money is viewed in "non-Western" cultural contexts. Illicit funds are an integral part of the functioning of the global capitalist economy. Annual profits from drug trafficking alone have been estimated to account for up to 5.5 percent of world GDP, or US$2.1 trillion.[4] As the anthropologist Carolyn Nordstrom (2007: 24) writes, illegal funds "aren't the exceptions to the rule of economy. They are the economy." And for this reason, the flow of trade cannot easily be categorized or separated into dichotomies such as legal/illegal or formal/informal.

This means that the physical properties of money, the materiality of illegally obtained cash that needs to be moved from one place to another, are inseparable from the kinds of interactions that make financial transactions possible. Indeed, in 2008 Antonio Maria Costa, then head of the UN Office on Drugs and Crime, claimed that the proceeds of organized crime were in many instances the only liquid funds available to banks on the brink of collapse during the financial crash of 2008.[5] He told reporters that "interbank loans were funded by money that originated from the drug trade and other illegal activities" and that "there were signs that some banks were rescued that way."[6] As a result, the majority of these funds were absorbed into the legal system. Therefore, when speculative capital markets imploded, it was "drug money—truckloads of cash, actual physical money," as the journalist John Gibler (2009: 33) wrote, that would become one of capitalism's "global savings accounts."

It was surprising to me at first that people in Santa Ana seemed unperturbed by Don Emmanuel's multiple identities and positionings as a fish buyer, money launderer, and former priest. In particular, his religious inclinations and his associations with organized crime seemed counterintuitive.

However, many rural Mexicans in the north are extremely devoted to Catholicism, and many of the drug cartels' most senior members as well as their most lowly underlings are from

Figure 7. Men pray at a shrine to Saint Jude. Photo by author.

very religious communities. Among the people I knew best, at the fringes of the drug trade, this religiosity was manifested most clearly in a sincere devotion to particular patron saints. There are a set of folk saints that are known for being popular among narcos and mules. In addition to Malverde, whose legacy I discussed in chapter 2, Santa Muerte, who is, among other things, the saint of "holy deaths," is known to be popular among narcos and mules. While these saints are made holy by popular belief, and condemned by the Catholic Church, Saint Jude, the saint of lost causes and a legitimate patron saint of the church, has also come to be associated with narco-culture. In many remote narco-routes through the northern deserts of Mexico one finds shrines to Saint Jude, or other folk saints, where smugglers stop to offer candles and prayers (see figure 7).

Drug traffickers are also well known for contributing money to and funding infrastructure improvements for churches.[7] For example, a recent church built in Hidalgo, Mexico, had a plaque engraved on a wall outside identifying the benefactor: Heriberto Lazcano Lazcano, a top leader of Los Zetas, one of the most powerful and ruthless Mexican cartels. Cartel members often seek out priests for spiritual guidance and redemption. Some priests accept large payments to perform baptisms, weddings, and other ceremonies for drug lords. In a famous case, an evangelical cartel called La Familia trained its employees to abstain from narcotics themselves and to study a special bible written by the gang's spiritual leader, which borrows texts from both the Old Testament and popular Mexican folk culture.[8]

Officially, the Catholic Church condemns drug trafficking. The archdiocese in Mexico has warned parishes not to accept dirty money, even if it's to pay for "good deeds." However, other members of the church have justified the use of narco-funds. In 2005 the bishop of the city of Aguascalientes claimed that "when the money is used for good works, it is purified."[9] There has also been speculation about more formal links between the church and the cartels. In September 2003 Cardinal Juan Sandoval of Guadalajara was investigated on suspicion of money laundering, but the investigation was dropped, purportedly due to lack of evidence.[10]

Of course, Don Emmanuel's simultaneous commitment to his religious ideals and his illicit business activities was much more incidental than some of the above cited examples. The point that I wish to highlight is not that the church is also complicit with cartel activities but that, like the military, the police force, and other institutions, it cannot be separated from the drug trade any more than other institutions embedded in the same financial networks. The same can be said for the identities generated by these institutions. That the multiple identities of Don

Emmanuel did not create dissonance in how he was perceived among local people is further evidence of how deeply penetrating the networks woven by organized crime are in the everyday lives of rural people in Mexico.

In fact, there was only one occasion when I heard someone criticize the double standard implied in Don Emmanuel's claiming to endorse the path of God. Isabella exclaimed one day in passing, "Don Emmanuel is such a hypocrite." Because that seemed to me the perfect way to characterize him, I was interested to hear her elaborate on this point. "Go on," I said eagerly, already nodding my head in agreement. "For example," she said, "he talks about how the body is a temple and is sacred, but it's not like he's such a saint. I mean, you saw him out with us the other night, right? He was drinking. He was sitting right there drinking a beer just like the rest of us. He's such a hypocrite."

This came as an anticlimactic twist to her series of observations. "That's what you mean?" I said. "I thought you were referring to the fact that he's involved with money laundering." I added that I thought it was strange that a former priest would be mixed up in something like that. Isabella rolled her eyes at me, "Ahh, *amiga*," she said, a little patronizingly. "Welcome to Mexico."

SIX

"Now They Wear Tennis Shoes"

Don Emmanuel used duct tape to strap the stacks of bills around Andrés's chest and stomach. He went once around tightly, just with the tape, and then he lined up the bundles of bills close together so that the second round of tape went over them smoothly. When Don Emmanuel finished meticulously taping the cash, Andrés put his undershirt back on and then his freshly ironed long-sleeved shirt, his good blue one with the stripes. He buttoned himself up and looked in the mirror. His body looked just the same, the layers of cash just slightly augmenting his contours.

Andrés explained that he started working for Don Emmanuel as his driver and all-around assistant. He took him to and from meetings and accompanied him on business trips. Andrés said that at first he thought Don Emmanuel might be gay. On the way back from some business in Tijuana, they stayed at a hotel and he invited him to sleep in the room with him. He was scared about accepting the offer. But he didn't want to sleep in the car either. In the end, he went in and was relieved to find that there were two beds. They sat on their own beds in their undershirts and watched TV for a few hours. Then they went to sleep. Nothing happened. The next day, Don Emmanuel woke Andrés early and said that he was going to need him to help hide some cash because they would be going through a checkpoint later that day. They would need to hide the money on his body.

After Andrés recounted this first trip through a military checkpoint with a load of money, I asked if he was scared. He said no. But then he went on to explain that he was "very uncomfortable." He had never had to smuggle anything on his body before, because when he had smuggled drugs they were always hidden somewhere in the vehicle. As they approached the checkpoint, he started having trouble breathing. Not because he was scared, he said, but because the cash felt "heavy." It put a lot of weight on his chest. In his whole life he had never seen as much cash as he had right then, taped to his body. But he knew it was just paper, so he thought maybe they had wrapped the tape too tightly around his ribs. He wondered if he was going to pass out from lack of oxygen. But he didn't. The soldiers made them get out of the car and checked it. But they didn't check Andrés's body.

Andrés was impressed by how smooth and professional Don Emmanuel was as they passed through the checkpoint. He said the soldiers asked where they were coming from, where they were going, and if they had any weapons. Don Emmanuel answered calmly and politely in his educated Spanish. The soldiers asked to look through the trunk and checked out the backseat.

"But weren't you afraid they were going to catch you?" I pressed. Andrés looked defensive. "No," he said flatly. "Why not? You could have gone back to jail," I said. Andrés shook his head, "No, it wasn't mine. The money wasn't mine." I asked why he decided to work for Don Emmanuel. "I thought you wanted 'out,'" I said. Andrés looked puzzled. "What do you mean 'out'?" he asked, not seeming to know what I was talking about. "Remember, you said you thought it wasn't worth the risk working for the mafia? When you first got out of jail?" He nodded. "But Don Emmanuel is not the mafia," he said. "He works *lavando dinero* [laundering money]. You know what that is, right?" I said of course I did, but Don Emmanuel was very likely working for drug traffickers, so Andrés was too if he was working for Don Emmanuel. Andrés just shook his head. "By that logic, everybody is working for the mafia," he said dismissively.

I asked about what had happened with his work at the restaurant. He said he had stopped working there because the restaurant mostly catered to private parties that were usually for mafiosos. In fact, in the city, he explained, most of the good restaurants are owned by high-earning narcos. Some of the parties were huge, with lots of food and people and copious amounts of drugs and alcohol. A few times he had made up to US$400 just from the tips. But he said it was dangerous because sometimes there were shootouts and fights at that kind of party, and he said he was back behind the counter in that open kitchen like a fool, practically waiting to get in the cross fire. He assured me that, if anything, working for Don Emmanuel was safer. And he was making more money.

In the process of explaining why it was safer working for Don Emmanuel, Andrés highlighted a crucial aspect of the transition from his life as a former narco. Getting out of the business of being a narco meant working just several steps removed from the networks that control illegal trade on the border and from the violence. But it did not mean that he had gotten out of the drug trade entirely, for the trade was too pervasive.

Andrés drew attention to the fact that illicit and licit activities are not entirely separate spheres and that this has implications for the ways local participants assess the risk involved in working in the drug economy. Drug trafficking organizations are amorphous, complex, and multifaceted, often acting as shadow governments in the areas they control, collecting "taxes" on local businesses and taking a percentage of the profits. Andrés was pointing to the messy ways in which many parts of the legal economy pander to and are sustained by the business of narcos. He implied that working in a restaurant in a border city such as San Luis means working for capos or, if not, for people who paid "taxes" to them. Either way, a higher-end restaurant such as the one Andrés worked in would have catered to people in the trade, and, as he pointed out, those were the customers who paid an enormous percentage of his wage.

The drug trade is such an integral part of the U.S. and Mexican economic systems that in high-traffic areas there are few lines of business or facets of government that have not been interwoven with it in some way. As discussed in the previous chapter, in the north even churches are built by narco funds or heavily subsidized by donations from drug cartels. Being "in" or "out" of the trade depends on how you're defining where the trade's boundaries are. For many people in northern Mexico there isn't really an "outside," and therefore the levels of risk that people assess are not measured in terms of being in or out. Andrés justified his new line of work in terms of physical safety. That is, he weighed the level of physical safety against the incentive of financial gain.

The anthropologist Mary Douglas (1992) defines "risk" as an estimation of possible events and a specific way of assessing and categorizing the social world. She has argued that the perception of risk does not involve simply the identification of objective outcomes but is rather a social and cultural process in which some risks are emphasized while others are ignored. This understanding of risk is helpful in making sense of the kinds of dangers working-class people expose themselves to in their involvement in the lower levels of the drug trade.

One of the common questions I am asked when I talk about the effects of the drug trade in northern Mexico is why people like Andrés, and others who have worked smuggling drugs or money in Mexico, would take such a risk. For most people who are even remotely aware of the violence devastating Mexico, there is an underlying assumption that even abject poverty could not make the financial incentive worth the potential dangers involved in such work.

While we have seen that there is a larger cultural and political context in which such work is experienced by the men and women I write about, calculations of risk are indeed a fundamental aspect of how they understand themselves in relation to the trade. They are not calculations made in a social vacuum guided by pure economic considerations about potential gains in relation to the risk of a jail sentence or even death. Rather, they are risks people weigh against the debts they owe their friends, the safety of themselves and their loved ones, the fact that their families may not have food to eat every day, and their sense of self-worth.

In this chapter, I come back to the stories of some of the central people whose experiences this book discusses by paying attention to how perceptions of risk factored into the decisions they made and the way they understood their positions within larger networks. I address the ways the concept of risk is related to the fuzzy boundaries of what can be identified as the drug trade in an economic and cultural context in which illicit and licit activities are intertwined.

"HE WON'T KILL YOU FOR FREE!": NARCOS, ASSASSINS, AND *LOCOS*

By one of my more recent trips to Mexico, in 2012, "risk" had taken a central place in my own considerations about fieldwork. I could no longer take a Greyhound into a border city such as Tijuana or Mexicali and then a handful of public buses out to the villages. Nor did it seem smart to hang around for someone I knew to pick me up, as I had done in the past. So I rented a car in L.A. and drove across the border. I also decided that instead of sleeping in one of the villages where I've stayed over the years, I would rent a trailer in Campo Blanco, one of the many little camps where Americans and middle-class Mexicans stayed on their way through the area to hunt or fish. Campo Blanco has about twenty trailers and houses, and I knew the man who runs the place, Edgar, whom I had met years earlier when Paz used to sell him tamales. Edgar tends to the property and guards it at night. For years, the middle-class Mexicans I knew in the region had been encouraging me to stay there instead of with "los pobres." They said I would be much safer in the guarded campo.

The families of Paz and Isabella all made a fuss about my new arrangement. They said I would be scared all alone in a trailer. But the trailer was right beside Edgar's house, and I was also a bit relieved by the prospect of not staying in Santa Ana, where I often felt overwhelmed by the living conditions and by social pressures and obligations. My first night there, however, I noticed someone following me on my way back to the campo from one of the villages. Initially, I thought whoever it was must be going to one of the colonias farther up the road. But when I made my last turn off the road and headed across an expanse of desert toward the jumble of trailers in the campo, so did the car behind me. I swerved to the side and stopped so the car could pass, annoyed that it was tailing me. But instead of passing the car pulled up beside me and stopped. I peered through the window as the man at the wheel glowered at me. I recognized him. I had seen him around in Santa Ana and had met him in passing with a group of people in Sauzalito at the festival for the Virgin of Guadalupe I had attended years before.

Scared now, I started driving again and pulled up right in front of Edgar's house. The lights were off. I honked a few times as I watched the man get out of the car behind me and walk up to my window. My doors were locked, windows up. He was smiling at me. I honked again and then rolled down the window a quarter of an inch to hear what he had to say. "I followed you," he said, with a glitter in his eye. "Yes, I noticed," I said flatly, and I rolled the window up, saying, "Okay, *buenas noches.*" He didn't move away from the window. He knocked on it and said through the glass, "I scared you." With the engine still running, I honked the horn again, still trying to get Edgar's attention. The man climbed back into his car and drove away, just as Edgar's light came on and he shuffled out of his house still half asleep. After telling Edgar what had happened, I bolted myself into the trailer for the night.

"I told you so," Paz said the next day. When I described the man, she knew who I was talking about. She said he was "crazy." Later Andrés corrected her, saying that he was actually called "El Loco" (the Crazy One). He explained that was his nickname. "Yes, but why is that his nickname?" I asked. "Well, he's kind of crazy," he continued. "He's killed a lot of people. Or they say so, anyway." I asked, "He's a narco?" "No," Andrés said without much certainty. "I don't think so. Just a hired hand." As he noted the expression of terror on my face, Andrés responded flippantly, "Don't worry, he won't kill you for free!"

Andrés and Paz assured me that the fact that El Loco was a killer had nothing to do with the fact that he followed me to the trailer. I had just made myself vulnerable driving alone at night. What was relevant for them was his "craziness"; that he worked as an assassin was incidental. It's also noteworthy that Andrés made a distinction here between an assassin and a narco. From his perspective, El Loco simply provided a fee-based service by contracting out rather than being a part of the drug organization itself.

This complemented Andrés's previous point about money launderers not being a part of the drug trafficking organizations they worked for. Assassins aren't necessarily a part of these organizations either. The distinction that Andrés made was consistent with recent research in the social sciences about the structure of drug trafficking organizations in Mexico. Specifically, some authors have criticized the term *cartels* because they are represented as being huge, highly organized entities that correspond neatly to territories and are removed from mainstream society. In fact, however, cartels are much more volatile and unstable than this representation, and many of the functions of a cartel are carried out by smaller, more loosely organized gangs as well as "cells," or groups and individuals such as outsourced growers, packagers, drivers, and warehouse guards (Astorga 2005; Campbell 2009).[1]

These networks also involve money launderers, chefs, and hit men like El Loco, all people neither directly part of the cartels nor outside their reach. As Andrés emphasized, to equate them in any way simply because they work for the same organizations would be misleading. In reference to El Loco, to me the difference seemed negligible at that moment. Either way, that night I was back in Santa Ana staying on Paz's couch.

SOCIAL DEBTS AND CALCULATED RISKS

The next day I drove into Mexicali with Paz and met Jorge. Paz had been dating him discreetly for a few months and said she thought she was in love. She wanted to go into the city to introduce us, and I was keen to drive away from there after the incident the previous night. My interactions with Jorge ended up furthering my understanding of how the dynamics of risk play out for lower-level participants in the drug trade.

Paz was nervous. Though she had been separated from her husband for over twenty years, she was worried about how people might perceive her now that she was in a new relationship. "What would Don Emmanuel think?" she giggled. "And Andrés would be so angry!" she said, with less glee. Paz knew that her son Andrés was working for Don Emmanuel, and she knew as well as everyone else what Don Emmanuel did for work. But it seemed that she didn't know how similar this work was to what landed Andrés in jail the first time. Paz had too much respect for Don Emmanuel to worry that he might be putting Andrés in danger. Besides, she was busy wondering how he might judge her.

On the way into the city, she told me more about Jorge. She had known him for the past few years because she had met him in jail when Andrés was there. He was Andrés's friend, so he had introduced them in the visiting area. Jorge had been caught smuggling a load of marijuana across the border in the tires of a car. He had been out of jail for two months. Now he was helping his mother repair her house in Mexicali and was looking for a job. "How long do you think until he gets back into his old work?" I asked, feeling cynical after my conversation with Andrés about his new job smuggling money. She shook her head. "Six years is a long time to be in jail," she said. "He doesn't want to go back."

We arrived at Jorge's mother's house, the virtues of which, such as air conditioning and indoor plumbing, Paz had been extolling on the drive. It was in a barrio on the western outskirts of Mexicali. Jorge came out to greet us as we drove up. He was in his mid-forties, with salt-and-pepper hair and a slight paunch. His mother came out soon after. She was probably in her sixties, with short white hair. After a friendly welcome and introductions, the problem of my shiny white rental car became the focus of everyone's attention. Jorge said we couldn't leave it on the street for the night. He went over to see if one of the neighbors would let us fence it into their lot. No one was home, but he finally found a guy across the street who would watch it if we gave him two bucks. "He's a meth-head," Jorge said in a tone that was meant to be reassuring. I made a confused face, and he explained, "He's up all night anyway. So it's no trouble for him to watch the car."

When the car was safely stowed under the watchful eye of the meth-head we went into Jorge's mother's house for tea. Paz told Jorge that she wanted to go out to listen to live music somewhere later but that first we should visit with his mother. After an hour or two of talking over instant coffee, Paz went into the kitchen to help Jorge's mom clean up. At that time, an awkward interaction occurred between Jorge and me. In a nervous aside, he asked me if he could borrow 100 pesos (at the time just less than US$10). He explained that he could pay me back later that night, when the guy who worked for his friend showed up at the bar we were going to. The interaction put me on edge, but Jorge was clearly embarrassed to ask, and it wasn't very much money, so I "lent" it to him without much hesitation.

We said goodnight to Jorge's mother, and the three of us walked out into the vacant street to find a bar. There was a live band playing loudly next door, but Jorge said it was a private party. So we walked into a dingy cantina a few doors down instead. There were four or five people at the bar, a jukebox in the corner, peeling plaster walls, chipped linoleum floors, and Christmas lights draped around the liquor that was stacked behind the bar. There were two notably overweight men at the end of the bar and between them and us a very tall, attractive transvestite wearing a skintight black dress, with long hair and long manicured fingernails. She was drinking beer out of a glass and filling it periodically from the caguama she had by her side. Jorge nodded his head at everyone there. They were all regulars.

I tried to order drinks, but Jorge cut in aggressively and ordered a round of beers. Although the cantina was largely empty, the music was so loud we could barely hear each other talk. The transvestite was swaying back and forth singing along to the romantic ballad blaring out of the jukebox. The two men at the bar were annoyed. One of them got up to change the music. Paz got in line at the jukebox to make a selection as well. The transvestite's songs were over, and the men's picks came on in a cascade of tuba and accordion and gunshots scattered through the familiar sounds of a corrido. The transvestite looked irritated and walked over to the door, lingering there smoking cigarettes.

Meanwhile, Jorge complained affectionately that he hadn't seen Paz for a long time. It had been a couple of weeks because of her new job. Paz was no longer taking care of el viejito. It turned out that Greg had been killed in a bar fight and Linda and the old man had moved back to L.A. This caused Paz no end of worry, for she feared that Linda was not taking good care of him. Since they had left, Paz had been working as a cook for one of the road crews that was repairing the highway out on Route 5 (about an hour north of where her compadre Cruz was stationed). She made food for the fifty-man crew. Jorge couldn't believe how badly they paid her—$130 a week. And she was working all the time, out in the sun carting burritos and sodas through the traffic and around the dangerous equipment. "Better than minimum wage," Paz said. But this comment set Jorge off on a rant about how terrible it is that the government would pay its own citizens so badly. "The government shouldn't exploit people," he said. "They make money, and then they pay the lowest workers the worst wages." He looked truly livid, and concluded, "I wish she didn't have to work there."

I suggested, by way of changing the subject, that that kind of exploitation was common in many lines of work in the region, and I asked whether he didn't think that he was exploited in his former job. "Six years in jail is a lot of time for crossing somebody else's merchandise," I suggested hesitantly. I felt that it was okay to ask this because Jorge had been speaking frankly about his situation since being released from jail, back at the house with his mother. But he seemed irritated by my supposition. "No," he said brusquely. "It was totally different because when I worked crossing drugs I was taking a calculated risk." When he got a load across in a car successfully, he said, he could make several thousand in one day. Jorge explained that Paz has no choice in her situation because there aren't other employment options where she lives. "There's no calculation on her part," he said. "She knew in advance that she was going to get paid shit."

Public health experts, who use their own rubric of risk calculation to estimate the vulnerabilities of particular populations,
have argued that a disposition for risk falls along class lines.
This means that certain disadvantaged groups experience
higher levels of risk, illness, addiction, and death.[2] Jorge was
making a similar point. He was drawing attention to the way
Paz's work in the legal market left her exploited and exposed to
a variety of hardships. As Jorge pointed out, the willingness to
engage in a high-risk practice is not just a calculation but also a
commodity. This was the difference between Jorge's work and
Paz's. Jorge was treating his own acceptance of risk as a commodity that could be sold to drug trafficking organizations that
basically paid him for accepting the risk of crossing a load. In
contrast, Paz's acceptance of risk was built into her socioeconomic status, where she knew in advance that she "was going to
get paid shit."

As noted previously, perceptions of risk are determined both
by cultural values and by social relations. The significance of
social relations within Jorge's calculation of risk became more
apparent later in the conversation when he talked about how to
break the news to Andrés that he was in love with his mother.
Paz looked terrified and giddy at the prospect. Jorge talked
about how the friendships one makes in jail are different from
other kinds of friendships: the bonds are stronger, and the sense
of fraternity is deeper.

Then he went on to talk in general about the relationships of
dependency that one develops in jail. He said that if you have
money you can get anything. Drugs get smuggled in with the
tacos; people buy and sell cigarettes, porn, alcohol, favors from
the guards, everything you can imagine. And if you don't have
money you just end up owing people. Jorge said, "And then you

end up with all these favors that you owe people that you can't repay while you're in there. And then you get out, and then, you know, a few months or years later they end up getting out too and they show up and you have to repay your debts." While it wasn't clear whether Jorge was talking about something that happened to him, Paz looked conscious of what Jorge was implying. "That's how you get sucked back in," he said. And he sipped on his beer thoughtfully. "And there's no way around it because you owe your friends."

As Jorge made clear, risk is not simply weighed against financial gain. It's also weighed against social debts—what you owe your children, your friends, your partners, and those who have helped you before. This is a dynamic we've seen in previous chapters. When Lupita carried Don Emmanuel's money on her body on their trip up from Mexico City, it was a social debt that she weighed against the risk. She knew that what they were doing was illegal and therefore dangerous for her. But there was never any question that she would carry the money for Don Emmanuel. He was driving her home, all thirty-six hours. Neither Lupita nor Don Emmanuel doubted for an instant that she would help him get the cash up north. A similar calculation must have gone through Paz's mind when El Gordo asked her for the "favor" of keeping his packages for him at her home. It was not principally a financial transaction. Paz was thinking about Andrés and whether they would be able to get him out of jail, and she was thinking about how to maintain her relationship with El Gordo in the meantime.

It occurred to me as I listened to Jorge talk, and thinking back to these other calculations of risk, that many people get "involved" in the drug trade in part because it is far riskier *not* to. That is, many people have more to lose by not agreeing to participate. It would have been far more dangerous for Paz to say no to El Gordo, and it would have been unthinkable for Lupita to have refused to help with the cash that they would be carrying in Don Emmanuel's car anyway.

For many of the people I've described in this book, it is also riskier not to participate because ultimately they are already positioned in the drug trade regardless of whether they "choose" to take on the role of smuggling or stashing drugs. Think back to El Chibo, the truck driver I described in the introduction, and his rationale for deciding to smuggle his first load across the border. As a trucker he was already part of an industry that was so entangled in the drug trade that he had to be constantly vigilant that he was not caught taking a load unknowingly. From this perspective, he was already at risk. In deciding to take a load willingly, he was mitigating this risk through financial gain and additional control. It was more dangerous for him to smuggle a load he didn't know about for free than to get paid for one whose passage he could oversee.

Jorge ordered another round of beers before I could even finish my first beer, much less tell him I didn't want another. Then he did it again. Finally, María's pick came on the jukebox, "José José," and Jorge led her out onto the empty dance floor. As they danced and I sat and watched, surrounded by all our beers, I realized why Jorge had to borrow the 100 pesos. He needed the money to buy us beers at the bar. He couldn't show up at the bar with two women and have them buy their own beers. It didn't matter that I had a good job and a problematically shiny rental car. It would have looked bad in front of Paz. So, with my new perspective from the barstool, I could see how for Jorge, as awkward as it was borrowing money out of the blue from a friend of his new girlfriend, it was the better option. Jorge was calculating his risks again, and he didn't want to risk looking cheap in front of his woman and his friends.

It struck me that this was another awkward side effect of being a woman and doing fieldwork alone in Mexico. Instead of buying beers for my companions and research participants, I was lending them money so they could buy my beers for me. Of course, I was preoccupied with my own gendered identity because of Paz's interpretation of how I attracted the attention of the hit man the night before. Her understanding, that I had made myself vulnerable by driving alone at night, reminded me of Álvaro and his incessant protests about the oddity of a woman hanging around alone. After that first confrontation about not having a husband or a family, Álvaro took it upon himself to lecture me about this on almost every occasion that I saw him. "You married yet?" he would ask.³

I haven't mentioned Álvaro since the first chapter because he went to jail in 2008 and has been there since. However, I have talked to him on the phone on a number of occasions. He sometimes called when I visited his sister, and she always said, "Guess who's here? *La canadiense* [the Canadian]!" And then she would pass me the phone.⁴ In these conversations we mostly made small talk. But the last time I talked to him, many years after first meeting him, we repeated the same conversation about my still not being married. "Ayayay...What are you doing!?" he said, taking up the now-familiar tone. "You're wasting your life!" This time I reacted with less restraint than usual, no doubt emboldened by Álvaro's location. "Álvaro," I said. "You're in jail! And you're still telling me I'm wasting *my* life."

It was not a very empathetic comment, but fortunately Álvaro didn't take offense. He just chuckled and quickly clarified that he was actually having a "very productive" time in jail. He said that he was in a good wing as a result of his impeccable behavior and that he had met really good people and made amazing friends. From Álvaro's perspective, with only a few years left on his sentence, being imprisoned for narcotrafficking was not the most tragic of fates. At least compared to the lot of an unmarried woman.

While I had interpreted Álvaro's implicit comparison of the plight of unmarried women and that of inmates as an expression of misogyny, in retrospect I wonder if I may have been distorting his message. Throughout the course of all Álvaro's disparagement about my traveling and working alone he was also pointing out a fact. I was a "girl" alone in the desert "with a bunch of narcos," no family with me, no husband. He was pointing to the obvious risks that I was taking. It was what Paz herself said about my vulnerability driving alone to the trailer park at night. Therefore, Álvaro was pointing out the same risk that El Loco drew my attention to far more rudely, tapping at my window and asserting that he had indeed scared me.

Jorge and Paz came back from the dance floor, mercifully interrupting my mental replay of El Loco at my window the night before, and we finally headed home from the cantina. But that night I had trouble getting to sleep on the couch at Jorge's mother's house. At 3 A.M., the live band at the party next door was still playing corridos. I could hear Paz and Jorge in the next room—the headboard banging into the wall. Jorge's mother, who had been asleep for hours in the room next to the couch, was snoring. I wondered how she could sleep with all the noise, the headboard, the high-energy music, the tubas and accordions.

Corridos never sounded so grating and sinister to me as they did at that moment. I pulled the pillow over my head to muffle the noises, and with my ears covered I tried to hum out all the sounds. But it was no use. As one song ended, the bandleader's voice cut through my humming as he shouted from next door, "Puro pa'delante Mexicali!" ("Let's go Mexicali!") Then they started playing another song.

"NOW THEY WEAR TENNIS SHOES"

"You know what you should do?" Andrés said. "You should offer to write a corrido for some people from the mafia in Canada. That's what you should do!" This was how Andrés responded to my initial plans to write a book about narco-culture in Mexico. I had told him about a book proposal I was going to write for a competition that offered a contract and $10,000 to write a book about a public issue. Andrés thought this was a rip-off. "Why write a whole book for $10,000 when you could get paid up to $30,000 for writing a song?" he reasoned. Especially because I would have the Canadian corrido market cornered since there are no corridos in Canada.

Many of my companions and long-term research participants in Mexico had never seen the point of writing articles and books. When I was struggling to finish my dissertation years ago, Javier, Cruz's son, had said, "You know you can pay someone to write that for you, right?" But writing about narco-culture in a book seemed particularly unsuitable in their eyes. The preferred genre for describing narco-culture is not books but blogs, songs, telenovelas, and black market videos.

"What's the book going to be called?" Andrés asked.

"*When I Wear My Alligator Boots*," I said. We both laughed uncomfortably. "Remember your alligator boots? Why don't you wear them anymore?" I asked. In fact, I hadn't seen Andrés or Javier wear their boots or their cowboy hats. I assumed that was one sign that they finally wanted to distance themselves from narcos.

Andrés said, "Now they don't wear the alligator boots so much anymore. Now only the old narcos wear the boots."

"What do they wear now?"

"Now they wear tennis shoes."

Over the past decade, the style of dress associated with narcos in Mexico has changed quite dramatically. The chero look is still popular among the old guard. But as Andrés went on to point out, the new generation wears designer brands such as Abercrombie & Fitch and Ed Hardy. They wear ball caps and bling and Nikes, more closely mimicking the style of successful rappers. The chero look that used to index the frontier cowboy has been swept up and transformed by the rapid globalization of both the economic networks and the cultural forms that constitute the drug trade. In the process, local meanings associated with the narcotraficantes have become intermeshed with global images of gangsters.

Corrido music has documented and commercialized some of these changes, and music videos of corridos are a revealing example of some of this global intermixing. Gerardo Ortíz's music video "A la moda" is a prime example. The video features shiny cars, AK-47s, and expensive suits and glasses. The chorus repeats the following refrain: "Hugo Boss, Dolce & Gabbana and on his face Prada sunglasses. With a diamond Rolex and an armored pickup. Entering the luxurious hotel with his bodyguards." But notably, the actors in the video, including Ortíz, still wear big fancy cowboy hats and exotic leather boots, and the glint of bejeweled rosaries can be glimpsed under the collars of their designer suits. In short, despite the global appeal of their designer brands, the touch of the chero is unmistakable.

The lineup of captured narcos that is presented to the media has also become a quintessential moment for the global distribution of narco-culture. Often, famous capos aren't well photographed until the time of their arrest. The photos published in the media are sometimes the first time the public puts a face, and an outfit, to the stories of their brutal exploits. Over the years, the lineup photos have instigated full-scale fashion rages. For example, when Edgar Valdez Villarreal (aka "La Barbie") was finally captured in 2010 after eight years of being hunted by Mexican and U.S. authorities, he was paraded in shackles wearing a Ralph Lauren "Big Pony" Polo shirt in green with "London" emblazoned on the front. Within a three-month period, seven high-ranking drug traffickers were arrested wearing open-neck, short-sleeved jerseys with the recognizable horseman-with-a-stick insignia. Now those shirts are everywhere in street market stalls all over the north of Mexico, sold for 160 pesos ($13.50) and clearly pirated by unlicensed vendors.

The diversification of aesthetic identifications among members of drug trafficking organizations has made the efforts to identify what a narco looks like all the more problematic. This is happening at a time when efforts to distinguish who is "in" or "out" are increasingly made by both law enforcement authorities and laypeople. Because of the increase in violence in the southern border region of the United States, believed to be attributable to the expansion of criminal operations over the border, intelligence and law enforcement agencies are requesting information on ways to identify those involved with drug trafficking organizations. An unclassified intelligence alert that was distributed to U.S. law enforcement in 2011 warned, "A proper narco is believed to sport a big sombrero and a decorative buckle. As for sneakers, narcos believe they are for mules and low-level assassins. A real narco wears cowboy boots and is seen more as a rancher or cowboy. A narco's boots are also the most decorative part of his outfit. Exotic animal skins, fancy stitching and garish colors are common. Narcos dress like cowboys who wholesale drugs and in their eyes gangsters dress like professional athletes who retail drugs."[5]

The compulsion to find ways to identify who is in the drug trade and who the "real" narcos are is also present locally: Esperanza in her village tracing the movements and activities of her neighbors, or Javier and Andrés delineating the "real" narcos from the "fakes." But the ultimate futility of such efforts was expressed most succinctly by a twenty-six-year-old taxi driver I met from Monterrey, Nuevo León. He said, almost apologetically, that he ends up driving narcos around in his taxi all the time. You can't help it, he explained. "You don't get to choose what people you pick up. And you can't tell anyway because they could be anyone, *niños y viejitos* [children and old people], working as narcos." Many of the people he picked up worked as *halcones* (lit., "falcons"; lookouts). "And they get into the car and start talking to me about their problems. They tell me all sorts of things, and they talk on their cell phones right in front of me. They say things like, 'Wait there in the house because the military just passed by.'"

The taxi driver doesn't get to choose whether to give rides to people working for the cartels because he can't tell who they are; they could even be little kids or old people. Then in the process of just doing his "legal" job he learns all kinds of highly volatile information. He learns where the stash houses are that the halcones are watching, he learns which military units the cartels are attempting to avoid, he learns their strategies for avoiding them, and he gains an understanding of how the organization is sustained by low-level lookouts. "But I'm just a taxi driver," he emphasized.

Some people have asserted that the attempt to clearly demarcate who the narcos are and where they go is one of the ways that a terrorized public has tried to deal with the risks of living in Mexico. A blogger from Guadalajara recently made fun of the way people constantly reassure themselves about the identifiability of narcos. "Do narcos pop the collars on their Versace polos, cruise about in gleaming Mercedes and jump the lines outside the best clubs in town?" he asks rhetorically. "No," he answers. "Those are the med students whose fathers paid for their schooling. Do narcos wear bandanas and combat boots and brandish machine guns while driving around in giant black trucks that have stylized silver wolves painted down their sides? No, those are just the state police."[6]

But as local cultural forms merge and are transformed by global associations with organized crime, the integration of economic networks has become increasingly noticeable. In fact, the constant representation of narcos as Mexicans hides the fact that a huge percentage of the profits of the drug trade go to the United States, not just to the criminal syndicates but also to major financial institutions and their shareholders. Recently money-laundering schemes have come to light in some of the major American financial institutions, including the well-known cases of Wachovia and Citibank.[7]

In December 2012 HSBC admitted to laundering billions of dollars for drug cartels (from Mexico and Colombia, among other places). The Justice Department decided not to press criminal prosecutions of the bank and instead opted for a financial settlement that amounted to about five weeks of income for the bank, $1.9 billion.[8] Its rationale for not criminally prosecuting the individuals in charge was quite simply because putting executives from such a critical institution in jail would be too destabilizing to the financial system. As the *New York Times* put it, authorities decided not to indict HSBC because "criminal prosecution would topple the bank and, in the process, endanger the financial system."[9]

One blogger succinctly characterized U.S. media representations of the war on drugs: "The American media regales the public with fairy tales of heroic 'warriors' doing battle with murderous gangsters named 'Joaquín,' 'Jorge' and 'Amado.' The fact is, more likely than not, the real narcos taking the biggest cut from deep inside the reeking abattoir of the grisly trade have far less prosaic names like 'Brett,' 'Ethan' or 'Jason.'"[10]

The juxtaposition of the "Amados" and the "Ethans" among the narcos draws attention to another fault line along which risk is distributed in the war on drugs. Risk doesn't just fall along class lines. It falls along national lines. There is no more obvious example of this than in the distribution of risk involved in the prohibition of drugs. Prohibition is ultimately a transfer of many of the risks involved in the production, smuggling, and trade of drugs from the consuming to the producing countries.[11] This is not to say that the drug trade and current drug policies have not wreaked havoc on American soil as well. The effects of drug addiction and gang violence have been devastating across the United States. Both the United States and Mexico have approached the drug problem in their own countries by criminalizing particular groups of people. In both cases, state agencies have targeted the poor; in the United States, they have predominantly targeted poor black men.[12] As Juanita Diaz-Cotto (2005) has pointed out, however, what makes the U.S. approach to the war on drugs unique is that it criminalizes not just the poor but also entire nations in Latin

America. In Mexico, this criminalization has played out in systematic destruction and mayhem that has resulted in unprecedented numbers of tortures, deaths, and disappearances.

It was a long drive back to Santa Ana from Mexicali the day after Paz and I spent the night at Jorge's mother's house. We were both tired and didn't talk much. But at one point, Paz turned to me and said, "So, how long until you think he gets back into the trade?" She was referring to Jorge, reversing the question I had put to her somewhat thoughtlessly the day before. I shrugged, and she smiled sadly.

What was becoming evident was that Jorge, like Andrés, had never gotten out of the trade. He was enmeshed in a web of relationships of obligation and debt to his mother and now to Paz, whom he clearly wanted to support, and also to the network of men he had become close to in jail. But he was also enmeshed in a larger, less visible system of relationships of obligation and debt with the "Bretts" and "Ethans" and the U.S. and global institutions that undergird the illegal economy. He was already positioned in this economy on the wrong side of the border fence. For while Mexico exports the drugs and profits to the United States, the United States exports the guns, the bloodshed, and the blame to Mexico.

Puro pa'delante Mexico

On August 12, 2012, a bus full of Mexican men and women who were victims of the war on drugs crossed the border at Tijuana to start a monthlong caravan across the United States. Many of them had lost loved ones to drug-related violence. Others had fled from bloodshed or been forced out of their communities. They were bringing with them across the border "a message of pain" to the American people.

The bus crossed into the vacant desert stretch at the border where the victims got out to begin their journey in a park in San Diego just beyond the border crossing. This is the same spot where in the 1880s a monument was erected to commemorate the initial point of the boundary and celebrate the friendship between the two countries. In 1971 Pat Nixon, wife of then-president Richard Nixon, named this place Friendship Park, or Parque de la Amistad. It was a place where friends and family could meet. People on opposite sides of the border, such as families separated by deportation, were able to touch and pass objects through the barrier made of vertical metal bars.

Figure 8. Border fence at Friendship Park. Photo by author.

Until 2009 a single chain-link fence separated the United States from Mexico at this stretch of the border. In mid-2009, however, U.S. officials closed the park to build an additional border fence, which severely limited access to it. And in early 2012, a new twenty-foot steel wall was constructed, which now cuts off all communication between the two sides at Friendship Park (figure 8). Therefore, this dramatically divided space was an ironic site for the Peace Caravan to begin its journey on U.S. soil.

There, beneath the tall, ominous, double-fenced border wall and the even more sobering sight of Tijuana's squalor and poverty beyond, press and supporters gathered on both sides of the border to welcome the Caravan. Amid the few dozen border guards circling the crowd, Javier Sicilia, the poet who was the instigator of the tour, told the press the purpose of their journey:

Figure 9. Protesters from the Caravana de la Paz, Los Angeles, California. Photo by author.

"We will travel across the United States to raise awareness of the unbearable pain and loss caused by the drug war, and of the enormous shared responsibility for protecting families and communities in both our countries" (see figure 9).

Sicilia became an activist in 2011 after his twenty-four-year-old son, Juan Francisco Sicilia, was found dead with six others, crammed inside a car outside the city of Cuernavaca. This violent incident fortified growing public criticism of the government discourse of impunity that has been characterized by the constant dismissal of "drug-associated" deaths as simply "cartel violence." The Peace Caravan to the United States emerged from a larger social movement that has formed over the past several years in Mexico calling for an end to the war on drugs. The Movement for Peace with Justice and Dignity (Movimiento

por la Paz con Justicia y Dignidad) is gaining a growing following through organized marches and rallies that have traveled
through Mexico and more recently the United States.

The movement has protested both drug war policies and the
government response to the violence and impunity created in
part by such policies. In 2008 Mexico's National Human Rights
Commission (CNDH) estimated that the impunity rate for
murder—that is, the rate at which murders are not investigated
or prosecuted—is as high as 99 percent.[1] In 2010 another Mexican research institute calculated that, in fourteen of Mexico's
thirty-one states, the chance of a murder leading to trial and
sentencing was less than 1 percent. And since then, experts say,
attempts at reform have stalled as crime and impunity have
become even more rampant.[2]

The ideological discourse that has justified the Mexican government's unwillingness to investigate the majority of these
murders is that the deaths simply consist of "criminals killing
each other off." As Gibler (2011: 41) wrote, "If you are found dead,
chopped up, wrapped in a soiled blanket left on some desolate
roadside, you are somehow to blame.... The very fact of your
execution is the judgment against you, the determination of
your guilt." Almost all the people I have met over the years who
have lost a loved one, whether disappeared or found murdered
and mutilated, have received the same response from the police
and the government: "They must have been involved."

On several occasions, erroneous government and media
claims dismissing violence as "narco-related" have come to
international attention. For example, in February 2010 gunmen
massacred fourteen teens at a party in a private home. The violence was quickly dismissed publicly by then-president Calderón, who claimed that the teens must have been narcos and that

the violence appeared to be the result of "a rivalry between gangs."[3] Protests immediately erupted in the city as the families of the victims refuted the accusation. The protests gained momentum as activists joined the families and participated in spontaneous press conferences that received international media coverage. Finally, Calderón apologized publicly at a meeting with the protesters, stressing that "the youth were athletes and students...not narcotraficantes" after all.[4] But the protests had become about a larger context of impunity surrounding the drug wars. Several mothers of the victims stood with their backs to the president. The crowd erupted into applause when one woman yelled out, "Enough with your war!" (Wright 2011: 725).

The members of the Peace Caravan and the movement for peace have cited repeated examples in which those killed, maimed, or disappeared in narco-associated violence had nothing to do with the cartels. These arguments have drawn attention to the hypocrisy of official claims that all the murders taking place in Mexico since the militarization of the war on drugs are narco-related when only 1 percent of the murders are actually investigated. It also draws attention to the fact that the U.S. and Mexican war on drugs is not just targeting drug dealers and cartel members, but is subjecting an entire population of ordinary citizens in Mexico to horrific violence and untold suffering.

But this critique does not address the underlying assumptions at work in the government's position that are equally problematic. The critique takes for granted that those "involved" can be clearly distinguished from those "not involved" in the first place. Instead, what has become clear from my ethnographic analysis is that the very distinction between those who are and are not involved is complicated by the profound interlocking of legal and illegal sectors and by the web of social and economic connections that characterize everyday life in the borderlands. Take the taxi driver from Monterrey, for example. Is he "involved" because he gives rides to lookouts? He knows more about the high-level operations of the drug trade than most mules, but he is just a taxi driver. Or Lupita's husband, Antonio, the award-winning military officer. Is he "involved" because he decided not to capture and imprison his uncle when he caught him with a load of drugs? If Lupita, Antonio, or the taxi driver were to die, it seems to me that their deaths could far too easily be written off as "involved" by officials and journalists while the realities of their involvement are far more complicated than such a dismissal would imply.

I have devoted much of this book to exploring how the everyday experience of people living in the borderlands complicates the very question of where the boundaries of the drug world begin and end. I hope that the stories I have told have also complicated the notion that the lives and deaths of those people who have indeed chosen to work directly in the drug trade are really so easy to dismiss. Andrés, Jorge, El Chibo, Álvaro, and many of the others I have described here chose to work in the trade, even if not under circumstances of their own choosing. Ultimately, if they become casualties of the war on drugs, their involvement should not be a rationalization, or a consolation. No death justifies maintaining a set of policies that have proven to be a failure. And the prohibition of drugs, and the "war on drugs," is nothing if not an utter failure.

In this book I have argued that drug trafficking activity, rather than being strictly localized in a tightly formed identifiable facet of organized crime, is amorphous. It is embedded in social relationships and inseparable from the daily rhythms of everyday life. It is intertwined with those sectors of the economy that are considered legal. This necessarily transforms our understanding of how people come to "choose" to get involved in the trade as well as under what circumstances some men and women are willing to risk so much to work as smugglers. This also has important implications for how we can even conceptualize what a "war on drugs" could mean under such circumstances. More specifically, it has implications for how we can understand such a war as anything other than a full-on attack on the Mexican poor.

In Friendship Park, I climbed on the bus with the victims I had just met. Men and women who had lost their sons and daughters and grandchildren, women who had lost their husbands. Twenty cars followed along behind, plus another bus of scholars and supporters. We drove up Route 5 toward San Diego. This route runs all the way from Mexico to Canada. This is the same Route 5 on which, a couple hundred miles farther south, Paz was probably distributing burritos amid the traffic; where farther south Cruz was probably still pacing around the road equipment or sitting on top of his bulldozer. Neither of them has ever been up this road beyond the border. Many of the people on the bus had never been to the United States either. Suddenly, a half dozen people on the bus got up to snap photos out the west window, pointing their cameras amid a cacophony of lenses shuttering. I turned my head to see what they were taking shots of: shimmering suburbs, the wealthy neighborhoods that stretch south of San Diego, gleaming with riches that are all the more striking just past the visible poverty of Tijuana.

The people on the bus shared with me horrific stories of the violence and heartbreak their families had experienced. Their stories were familiar to me from my time in Mexico, but the motley cast of characters following along to support the bus surprised me. Some were expected: academics, journalists, NGO and human rights workers. But others seemed less likely: a hip-hop artist from Colombia and a group of lawyers and law enforcement officers from the United States.

At the Los Angeles stop of the tour, I interviewed a former cop named Dean Becker. One of the people on the bus pointed him out, commenting in Spanish that he looked "like a real gringo." I noticed what was printed on his shirt: "Cops say legalize drugs. Ask me why." I approached him and asked, "Why?" He spoke confidently into my tape recorder: "I want to eliminate the reason that thirty thousand violent street gangs are prowling through our neighborhoods. I want to eliminate most of the reason for these violent barbarous cartels south of our border, and, additionally, I'd like to stop pouring money down the rat hole." His answer was so polished that it was obvious he had experience talking about the subject. Later he explained that he had been a security policeman in the U.S. Air Force for thirty years. He saw the failure of prohibition firsthand as he tried to enforce it. Now he runs a radio show out of Houston that covers topics related to the war on drugs. Dean is part of a growing group in law enforcement, along with James E. Gierach (see chapter 4), called LEAP (Law Enforcement Against Prohibition) that speaks out against the prohibition policies that fuel violence in the United States and Mexico.

The people involved in organizations such as LEAP and the Movement for Peace with Justice and Dignity suggest a broad new security strategy. Among other recommendations, they include, at a minimum, the exploration of alternatives to drug prohibition such as decriminalization;[5] an open discussion of drug policy reform that replaces the current criminal justice approach with a public health focus; a halt to the illegal smuggling of weapons across the border to Mexico; and concrete steps to combat money laundering, including closing loopholes and holding financial institutions accountable. They also call on the U.S. government to immediately suspend its assistance to Mexico's armed forces.

BEYOND THE BLOODSHED TO A LONGER VIOLENCE

The violence that has characterized the war on drugs goes beyond the tremendous bloodshed that has resulted from U.S. and Mexican government policies. The murders, kidnappings, and disappearances associated with drug trafficking organizations, the militarization of the region, the human rights abuses, and the widespread impunity and government corruption point to an underlying structural violence. The drug war reveals fundamental problems with the structures of economic and political systems. The cartels function as the quintessential neoliberal subjects: free market entrepreneurs. They maximize profits at *all* costs. And their huge profits are shared by thousands of legal institutions, banks, and individuals throughout the world. The war on drugs, in short, is a diagnostic site for the injustice and inhumanity of current economic and political systems.

For people like Paz, Andrés, and Jorge, what creates the fundamental vulnerability in their lives is not just the violent social conditions imposed by prohibition, but, ultimately, the underlying social insecurity that makes the drug trade one of the few sources of upward mobility. More than 51 percent of the

Mexican population live in poverty according to a 2009 World Bank report (Gibler 2009). By some estimates, up to 55 percent of Mexico's working population are employed in the "informal economy."[6] That is, like many of the people whose stories have become familiar in this book, the majority of Mexico's population works under uncertain conditions, without benefits or support. Therefore, the employment options that are available to people in rural villages such as Santa Ana are largely illicit, regardless of their involvement in the trade, since those options are still part of this underground economy.[7] They may work like Cruz, collecting scrap metal with a truckload of other men, or Andrés, piling rocks to make way for the development of roads through the region, or Paz, selling tamales out her car window. And some work at the fringes of the drug trade, catering the parties of narcos, driving them around, smuggling their merchandise, and laundering their money.

Therefore, the necessary and immediate redress to the violence generated by the drug trade in Mexico and the toll of drug addiction is to end prohibition policies and invest in viable public health options. In both the United States and Mexico, however, any attempt to fundamentally address the drug problem will have to also address the larger economic imbalance between the rewards of the legal economy and those of the underground economy. Likewise, long-term solutions will also need to focus on the political-economic roots as well as the ideological and cultural sources of social marginalization (Bourgois 2003: 327). In short, the social conditions that put people at risk of developing substance abuse problems are precisely the conditions that make them vulnerable to being drawn into direct involvement in the trade as small-time traffickers and mules.

A FAREWELL AMID INCOMMENSURABLE
RISKS

The last time I saw Andrés, we talked about this book again. He was packing his bag to head out on a business trip with Don Emmanuel, and I was sitting at their kitchen table drinking coffee. Elsa and the kids were watching TV on the couch, and Paz was out on the highway somewhere, distributing burritos. I told them I was still writing the book, and Andrés said, remembering our former conversation, "That's the one where you get $10,000 for a book?" "Right," I said. "But it turns out they are not going to give me the advance, just the book contract." Andrés snorted, "What?" "It's because the economy crashed," I said, "and the presses lost all their money." Andrés laughed out loud and shook his head. "Just like the mafia," he remarked. "They promise you a pile of cash to make a run, and then, when you make the delivery, they end up just giving you half because 'the economy is bad.'" Elsa, half watching telenovelas but always alert enough to make a jibe, said, "Yeah, but in this case they tell her she's not going to get anything. And they tell her *before* she makes the run." They both laughed and shook their heads.

Andrés kept shaking his head but stopped laughing. His expression changed as if he were just realizing the implications of their joke. "You're crazy. Aren't you scared writing about something like that? It's dangerous! You're not going to interview mafiosos, are you? You can't do that." He was leaning forward a bit menacingly, the contents of his duffel bag starting to spill out. "No!" I said defensively, taken aback by his change of tone. "The book is not about the cartels or mafiosos." I clarified, "It's about the everyday effects. You know, the music, the addiction, the notches in the desert, the clothing. It's going to be about normal people ..."

"Okay, but you can't interview the mafiosos," he repeated, maintaining his protective tone but having already lost interest in the topic as he turned his attention back to packing his bag and preparing to leave. It was noteworthy that Andrés quite suddenly became incensed about the dangers of writing a book like this, something we had talked about many times before. Once the immediate financial incentive was withdrawn from the equation, all he saw remaining was the risk. By Andrés's logic, which was not attentive to the academic obligations of publishing (essential to such processes as promotion and tenure), the advance for the book was the only grounds on which to justify putting myself in danger. My own calculus of risk was not comprehensible to Andrés in much the same way that the dangers he was subjecting himself to seemed reckless from my perspective.

At the time, I was irritated by his reaction, both because it seemed hypocritical and because I was indeed nervous about writing on the topic. "Why should I be scared?" I asked, and then continued sarcastically, "Why should I be scared, when you're the one strapping on thirty grand of Don Emmanuel's money. You're the one putting yourself at risk." I continued, expressing some pent-up disappointment about his new line of work, "What is he paying you? And think about what he gets out of it. It's not fair. You're being exploited." Andrés tuned back in to the conversation under the glare of my accusations. "No," he said calmly, shaking his head back and forth reassuringly and zipping up his duffel bag. "There's no risk. It's not a risk to me." I looked at him confused. "Why?" I asked. He continued, "Because it's not mine. I'll carry the money. But if they catch me, I'll tell them that it's not mine." It took a moment for the familiarity of this expression to sink in: that was what Andrés told himself as he waited to get out of jail the first time, what he told his mother, what his mother told herself. "That's what you said the first time," I muttered. He looked up with bemused recognition, shrugged, and with his duffel bag over his shoulder and his tennis shoes on his feet, he waved and made his way out the door.

In live performances, singers of corridos will often yell, "Puro pa' delante Sinaloa" (or "Mexicali" or "Chihuahua") as a shout-out to the place where they are performing. The crowd always cheers in response to this cry, which means "full ahead," a contraction of *puro para adelante*. When I asked Rafa, Paz's son-in-law, what the phrase meant, he said, "It just means 'Let's go!'" "But why do they say it?" I asked, hoping for a less literal answer. "It's just a thing they say to the crowd to get them excited." Anytime I came upon someone listening to corridos, I would ask about the meaning of the phrase, which seemed to capture much of the cultural and social allure of the genre.

Isabella said, "It means when you have to charge forward even when you are being attacked." Later I ran this definition past Isabella's older brother, Daniel. He agreed and elaborated: "It's like, there's no going back." Then, as an example, Daniel told me a story about when he crossed the border into the United States as an illegal migrant many years ago (he had since been deported back to Mexico). He said that when he and his companions came to the border crossing they hesitated. Finally someone in his group yelled, "Puro pa'delante!" and they all charged across at once.

Trying to refine my question, I asked Daniel, "Why do they always say 'puro pa'delante' in narco-corridos but not so much in other kinds of music?" He explained that it is like when someone gets into narcotrafficking and "you can't ever get out again." Later I asked Andrés the same question. His answer was, "Well, 'puro pa'delante' is like, you have to do something, good or bad. And you shouldn't regret what you have to do. And you have to do it well."

In a disturbing way, this sentiment describes the series of circumstances that many of the men and women I met have found themselves in. These are circumstances that are largely beyond their control and that shake this region like an earthquake. Both the drug trade and its violence overtake them. Think of Andrés bearing up, trying to breathe under all the weight at the military checkpoint, or of Paz slipping her last wad of cash into the guard's hand at the jail. Remember Lupita, stuffing her baby's diapers with hundred-dollar bills. Or Celia, the seven-year-old girl, adjusting the pink pom-pom on her full facial hoodie and posing for the camera. And don't forget Cruz, out there in the desert on top of his bulldozer, counting his way through earthquakes. Rather than regret their actions, they just try to do whatever they have to do, and try to do it well. It's not unlike Cruz's approach to surviving a real earthquake: bearing up and counting through the tremors until, eventually, the world returns to stillness.

NOTES

INTRODUCTION

1. See Gibler 2011; Tuckman 2012.

2. Methamphetamine is the drug that has had the most visible effect on the region, which I discuss in more detail in chapter 4. Mexican methamphetamine production has been increasing dramatically in the past few years since the U.S. government has tightened restrictions on the chemicals necessary for domestic production.

3. See Fayerick, Cary, and Steffen 2009.

4. According to Peter Andreas, who has written extensively on the connections between the drug trade and NAFTA, U.S. customs and drug enforcement personnel openly joke that NAFTA refers to the "North American Drug Trade Agreement" (Andreas 1996: 54). Andreas also points out that for these reasons NAFTA served as a scapegoat for opportunistic lawmakers who claimed that free trade was to blame for the failures of drug control and to lobby for even more resources for drug interdiction (13).

5. Several million trailer trucks cross the border each year (Burnett 2010; Gaouette 2011).

6. There are a variety of ways that smugglers find their targets for such operations. Often they post lookouts at border crossings to

identify vehicles using the express lane through a given port of entry. After identifying a vehicle, smugglers obtain the car's vehicle identification number and have spare keys made. Smugglers then covertly stash a load of drugs in the vehicle's trunk, and the next morning the owner drives the car across the border, unaware it contains drugs (Ovemex 2011a).

7. There have been reports of drug traffickers paying managers in trucking companies per pound for drug shipments successfully making it across the border (Burnett 2010). In other cases, Mexican truck companies reportedly pay for additional security to investigate and ensure that cartels don't stash drugs under or inside trailers (Andreas 1996).

8. See Burnett 2010.

9. While former president Calderón is often attributed with militarizing the war on drugs, the extension of military forces into the role of drug control was a longer historical process. The Salinas administration (1988–94), under pressure from the United States, had also made significant steps toward redefining drugs as a national security threat and expanding the role of the military in enforcement efforts (Andreas 1996: 55). Similarly, the concept "War on Drugs," a term first used by Richard Nixon in 1971 in the context of policies that his administration implemented as part of the Comprehensive Drug Abuse Prevention and Control Act of 1970, was a continuation of drug prohibition policies in the United States that started in 1914. For a timeline of drug war policies, see NPR's Drug War Timeline (2007).

10. See Wright 2011; Human Rights Watch 2011. See also the full report of Mexican attitudes toward human rights violations by the Pew Research Center (2012).

11. The concept of the war on drug is therefore misleading because the binational campaign, imposed by the U.S. government, is not one of a traditional military nature; instead, military operations pursue civilian traffickers. The anthropologist Howard Campbell (2009) has argued that the "war" metaphor is also disingenuous because it implies that the state and the traffickers constitute separate spheres. While the largest Mexican criminal organizations do maintain some autonomy from the state, the fact is that state and illicit activities are tightly interconnected. Drug organizations and gangs often work in

tandem with soldiers and government officials in ways that complicate the divide between the illegal and legal realms. For these reasons, Campbell (2009) has proposed the term *Drug War Zone* to refer to the constellation of "legal" and "illegal" actors and the shifting political and geographic terrain that constitutes the "war on drugs."

12. See the edited collection by Gaviria and Mejía (2011) for an extensive analysis of the economics of the drug economy. They show that in the case of Colombia 2.6 percent of the total street value of cocaine produced remains within the country, while 97.4 percent of the profits are reaped by criminal syndicates and laundered by banks in first world "consuming" countries. Beittel (2013) writes that, while the amount of money grossed by the drug trade in Mexico and the United States is estimated at between $20 billion and $30 billion, some experts in Mexico have remarked that the profit cartels in Mexico keep is likely in the $4 billion to $6 billion range.

13. See Bandow 2012.

14. See Duke 2009; *Economist* 2012; Davenport-Hines 2001.

15. As many have pointed out, the failure of alcohol prohibition in the United States (ending in the 1920s) should have been the first indication of the ineffectiveness of prohibition policies. The "noble experiment" was devised to "combat crime and corruption, and improve the health" of the citizens of America. But the results showed a complete failure on all counts (see NCLOE 1931).

16. The shifting networks and territories through which cartels transport drugs by bribing politicians, police, military officials, and border guards is often referred to as *"la plaza"* (Campbell 2009: 23). Many scholars trace the levels of corruption in the government in relation to the cartels to long-term corruption established during the reign of the Partido Revolucionario Institutional (PRI), which was the ruling political party from 1929 to 2009 and then returned to power with the election of Enrique Peña Nieto in 2012. The PRI made certain forms of corruption possible in part because of the hierarchical structures it established and also the endemic corruption of ruling elites. However, some have argued that during the party's first period in power drug-related violence was lessened by the fact that the relationships between drug traffickers and officials were relatively stable (Campbell 2009: 271).

17. For example, I came to know the truck driver El Chibo because he dated a close friend of mine, Isabella. When I decided to write this book, I sought out other truck drivers to interview them about how the trucking industry had been affected by the trade. I had met some truck drivers because they would come into fishing villages to pick up fish and others because they would stop in villages close to the main road to buy meth during long-distance hauls. The conversations I had with truckers after El Chibo often confirmed and elaborated bits and pieces of El Chibo's accounts (as did newspaper and Internet research), but very few of those I met were as open about the drug trade as El Chibo, and only a few offered accounts of their own smuggling activities. They helped to contextualize El Chibo's experience, but because I did not know them as well, the interviews were very different in quality.

18. Archival research was also a significant component of this project. In addition to my primary focus, the local-level impacts of the drug wars in Mexico, I followed national news on drug policies, cartel politics and conflicts, and U.S. interventions. For this component of my research, I regularly consulted the archives of local and national newspapers such as *La Voz de la Frontera, La Jornada, Processo,* and *La Crónica de Hoy.* Because of censorship, important media sources such as the blogosphere, in particular, el Blog del Narco and the Borderland Beat, have emerged that cover narco-related violence. This dual-level analysis has added an important perspective because national and international media coverage focuses almost exclusively on the violence and politics that have resulted from rival cartels battling over territories based in urban centers and on the border. The low-level effects of these conflicts for those at the bottom of the industry are rarely covered.

19. There are a number of rich ethnographic accounts of drug trafficking in Mexico and elsewhere that have served as invaluable guides to how to carry out and represent research on drug trafficking and addiction. For the Mexican case Howard Campbell's work has been crucial (see also Malkin 2001; McDonald 2005, 2009). In addition, Philippe Bourgois's (2003) seminal work on drug dealers in Harlem is indispensable (see also Bourgois and Schonberg 2009; Garcia 2010; Singer 2006, 2008).

20. See Beittel 2013.

CHAPTER I

1. The term *comadre* or *compadre* indicates the relationship of *compadrazgo* (coparenthood) between the parents and the godparents of a child. In Mexico, as in other parts of Latin America and Spain, compadrazgo is an important social institution that begins when a child is baptized.

2. Ana's family, like most of those I stayed with over the course of my research in the area, refused to accept money for my lodging. She insisted that I was her guest. One result of this refusal, however, was that I felt compelled to repay her in other ways, and giving her rides was one such simple favor I found difficult to refuse.

3. See Rosenberg 2010.

4. See Associated Press 2012.

5. See Booth 2012.

6. Maquiladoras have become the prevalent organization of labor in Mexico among transnational corporations. They consist of administrative and technical operations located in the United States and assembly sites located in Mexico due to its inexpensive labor (Dwyer 1994). These corporations import duty-free parts to be assembled in Mexico; the finished product is reexported to the United States. The maquiladora sector was originally created with government support in 1965 to stimulate investment and encourage industrial development at the border. With the implementation of NAFTA in 1994 the sector grew markedly, with a 40 percent growth in Mexicali alone.

7. Another reason that femicide is crucial for understanding the violence of the drug trade in Mexico is because the impunity, human rights abuses, and related government discourses on the murders are inseparable. The geographer Melissa Wright (2011) has argued that the effects of drug violence on women in northern Mexico is inseparable from the femicide. The government discourse on the violence of both spheres is very similar. Femicide has been dismissed as the murder of "prostitutes," and the drug violence has been depicted as "criminals killing each other off."

Wright has critiqued these discourses as being intrinsically masculinist. They hold together around a binary of masculine rationality, whereby on the one hand, business-minded criminals kill themselves off protecting their territory; and on the other, women governed by feminine irrationality live double lives as prostitutes and thus invite the violence unleashed on them. She argues that the binary is further reinforced spatially around men's violent business that happens in public on the streets, in contrast to women's promiscuous domestic activities in bedrooms. Therefore, contestation over the political meaning of the deaths in relation both to femicide and to the events called drug violence are deeply connected to the ways that space and violence are gendered.

8. These mothers draw on a long and powerful lineage of female-led activism against state terror in Latin America (epitomized by the mothers of la Plaza de Mayo in Argentina).

9. Martinez 2010. See also Diaz-Cotto 2005 on how the fastest-rising prison demographic in the West is women incarcerated for drug trafficking.

10. See Perez 2012.

11. See Wilkinson 2009.

12. The novel, which was later made into a popular telenovela, begins with twenty-three-year-old Teresa, a classic narco-wife, learning that her trafficker boyfriend has been shot and that his assassins are after her as well. Instead of ending the way so many narco-wives do, Teresa escapes her assassins and flees to Spain in a journey that involves a series of lovers who are all eventually killed. After a stint in jail, she makes her way up to the most powerful position in the drug trade. She becomes the "Queen of the South." Teresa survives through her masculine traits: sheer guts, shrewd intelligence, and a cutthroat business sense. Historically, there have been a handful of famous female drug lords, including "Lola La Chata" and "La Ma Baker" in Mexico City, "La Nacha" in Juárez, the Arellano Félix sisters of the Tijuana Cartel, Sandra Ávila of Sinaloa, and Zulema Trevino (see Campbell 2006).

13. Quoted in Kimpel 2009. Women such as Jenni fit into the formula of power achieved "outside the rules" as a form of rebellion against "traditional values" (Altamirano 2010; Mondaca Cota 2004). As Campbell (2008) points out, individual female "liberation" through

trafficking does little to transform a larger patriarchal cultural economy and may even reinforce it through the promulgation of misogynistic symbolism.

CHAPTER 2

1. This figure is based on a 2011 Council on Foreign Relations estimate (Rawlins 2011).

2. Some people I met from other areas of Mexico's northern border were skeptical that people in Santa Ana did not know which cartel they were working for or more generally living under the jurisdiction of. A taxi driver I met from Monterrey, Nuevo León, outright scoffed at the idea. "There's no way," he said. "They just don't want to say it out loud."

I took his point seriously since that conversation paid more attention to this issue. When the topic came up I sometimes pressed people on it, asking again which cartel was dominant in the area. While some people, like Andrés and Álvaro, specifically paid attention to these kinds of things, the majority, even mules like Jose, Octavio, and Isabella, did not know or expressed uncertainty. When I asked Isabella for the second or third time she called one of her boyfriends and asked him.

In part these differences result from how relatively contested a given territory is. Where there have been ongoing conflicts there have also been extensive public outreach campaigns on the part of the cartels, consisting in mantels *(narco-mantas)* hung in public places staking a claim to a territory and threatening rivals. The differences can also be accounted for by the remoteness of Santa Ana relative to urban centers and centers of cartel power.

In *El Sicario: The Autobiography of a Mexican Assassin,* by Molly Molloy and Charles Bowden, which consists of a collection of long interviews with a man who worked as an assassin in Mexico for several decades, a similar disengagement from cartel politics is evident. As a hired hand the assassin admits that at points he did not know precisely on whose behalf he was being hired (Molloy and Bowden 2011).

3. See Keefe 2012. Note, however, that this estimate encompasses only the amount cartels spend on bribing lower-level officials, like municipal police. Extravagant bribes have been reported for higher-

level government officials, like the former top antidrug federal prosecutor who was paid $450,000 a month to pass information to a cartel (Ellingwood 2008), as discussed in the previous chapter. Joaquín Guzmán was also reported to have paid $3 million to escape from a maximum-security prison in 1993 (Blackstone 2012).

4. This is a large area of interest in anthropology. See, e.g., Cattelino 2008; Clifford 2001; Gordillo 2004; Li 2000; Niezen 2003; Miller 2003.

5. I've written about these issues elsewhere (Muehlmann 2008, 2009).

6. See also Limón 1994.

7. For instance, Gutmann (1993) shows how in one colonia in Mexico City, women's increased involvement in paid labor and the growing participation of men in realms such as housework resulted in an erosion of male ideologies associated with machismo (see also Gutmann 1997; de Barbieri 1993; Irwin 2003; Valdes and Olavarría 1998; Viveros, Fuller, and Olavarria 2001; Viveros 1997).

8. This arrangement was formalized in the 1854 "Gadsden Purchase" (known as Venta de la Mesilla in Mexico), which is a region comprising present-day southern Arizona and New Mexico that was "purchased" by the United States from Mexico.

9. Formal interviews aren't always very helpful in anthropological research. This is especially the case when long-standing relationships are involved, when most topics might be more effectively discussed in casual contexts and gleaned from participant observation. But with Andrés I wanted to have the opportunity to ask more systematic and detailed questions, particularly in regard to his experiences in jail.

CHAPTER 3

1. See Wilkinson 2012.

2. Many scholars use the prefix *narco-* when referring to corridos that chronicle the drug trade (and to differentiate them from traditional corridos that tended to celebrate heroes of the Mexican Revolution, as I discuss later in the chapter). However, in contemporary Mexico "corrido" is usually used synomymously with "narco-corrido" (which in fact sounds redundant to locals in the contemporary context). I use

both here in order to sometimes highlight the distinction between contemporary corridos dealing specifically with drug trafficking.

3. See also Valenzuela Arce 2002; Quinones 2001.

4. For more on this interpretation of corridos, see Dávila 2011; Villalobos and Ramírez-Pimienta 2004; Wald 2002.

5. See Paredes and Bauman 2003; Ramírez 1990.

6. While there have been outright attempts to ban corridos from the radio and television, usually censorship is more indirect. Instead of laws against playing the music, there are agreements between the state governments and the radio and television programmers that they will "voluntarily" not play them. More recently, in 2011, Sinaloa issued a law threatening to rescind liquor licenses from bars that play corridos (Valdez-Cárdenas 2011). The state has since then fined and banned popular commercial bands such as Los Tigres del Norte from playing within city limits.

7. Quoted in Valdez-Cárdenas 2011.

8. See Ovemex 2011a.

9. See deBree and Worfolk 2009.

10. See Reyes 2012.

11. In contrast, in the United States similar debates about the harmful effects of music have been framed racially (McDonald 1988; Rosenbaum and Prinsky 1991). Amy Binder (1993) shows how in the United States public debates over the potential harms of violent lyrics were racialized. In contrast to heavy metal, where the media emphasized the harmful effects to the listeners (mostly white youth), rap music was portrayed as a "danger to society," implying that listening to the violent and misogynist lyrics would lead to rape and murder.

12. While this has become the commonsense view in North America on the effects of oversaturation to violent images, the position has also been explicitly theorized by various authors (Adorno and Bernstein 1990; McLuhan 1994).

CHAPTER 4

1. Angela Garcia (2010: 25) points out, writing about the United States, that while drug use has steadily increased in rural areas since 2000,

especially in the American heartland, the resounding tendency has been to focus studies of addiction on urban areas. She argues that despite this trend numerous reports have indicated that rural communities are especially vulnerable to meth addiction because of two primary factors: the relative ease of manufacturing the substance from common household goods (and ammonia, which is also used as fertilizer) and the abundance of wide open spaces where labs can operate undetected.

2. UNODC 2010.

3. The name of this song in Spanish is "Clave privada" (Private Code).

4. See Cuddehe 2011.

5. NDIC 2011:32.

6. James E. Gierach, interview by author, Chicago, September 3, 2012.

7. See Johnson 2012; Rosenburg 2012.

8. See Bourgois and Schonberg 2009; Singer 2008.

9. See Rydell et al. 1994.

CHAPTER 5

1. Estimates range between $10 billion and $45 billion per year (see Sarmiento and Gutierrez 2011). As with most estimates on the economics of the drug trade, this range reflects the indeterminacy of data on illicit economies more generally.

2. Of course, I did not know any of this at the time. I researched it later on the Internet and found a particularly helpful explanation, "How Money Laundering Works," on the website How Stuff Works: http://money.howstuffworks.com/money-laundering.htm.

3. See Castillo 2010.

4. UNODC 2011.

5. See Syal 2009.

6. Quoted in Saviano 2012.

7. See Cevallos 2011.

8. See Kocherga 2011; Grillo 2009.

9. Quoted in Cevallos 2011.

10. Cevallos 2011.

CHAPTER 6

1. For this reason, some scholars have preferred to use the term *la plaza*—the transportation route controlled by specific cartels in collusion with police, military, and government officials. This term is preferable because it refers to the intersection of traffickers and law enforcement authorities that control territories. It also highlights the ways that cartels do not represent a "parallel power" independent from the state but one promoted and protected by various sectors of the state (Astorga 2005; Campbell 2009).

2. See Blakely et al. 2004. For other work in the social sciences that has discussed the cultural dimensions of "risk" from a more critical perspective, see Beck and Ritter 1992; Giddens 1990; Miskimmin 2008.

3. I have omitted stretches of interviews like this here because they are largely irrelevant to the themes in question. But this example gives a fairly extreme case of the general kinds of gendered "white noise" that are often edited out of the final descriptions of ethnographic fieldwork. There are, however, quite a few anthropologists who have written about similar experiences. See, for example, Abu-Lughod's (2008) description of her reception as a grown woman without children among Bedouin women and her own process of feminization in the field (1988), Tsing's (2005) description of fending off being molested in a truck during her fieldwork in Indonesia, and Kulick's (2010) discussion of how his identity as a gay man facilitated his fieldwork among Brazilian transgendered prostitutes. The ways that gender bias more generally may have been manifest in early ethnographies has been discussed in anthropology as well (Keesing 1985; Weiner 1976).

4. As mentioned previously, I am a dual citizen and I lived in the United States for large stretches of this research. However, my research participants in Mexico all preferred to identify me as a Canadian. I imagine there were many reasons for this—many of which have been discussed in this book—but what most people articulated explicitly was that I didn't speak Spanish like a "gringa" and that I was born in Canada and, therefore, more Canadian than American in their opinion.

5. EPIC Gang Intelligence Unit 2011.

6. Johnson 2011.

7. See Vulliamy 2012.

8. See Taibbi 2012.

9. *New York Times* 2012.

10. Anti-Fascist 2012.

11. Gaviria and Mejía 2011.

12. For more on the racialized history of the American war on drugs, see Alexander 2010.

CONCLUSION

1. Human Rights Watch 2008.

2. See Cave 2012.

3. See Ellingwood 2010.

4. Quoted in Malkin 2010. See also Cardona 2010.

5. Some have argued that because drug cartels have diversified into various other realms of business, both legal and illegal (e.g., human smuggling, kidnapping, extortion, and oil theft), at this point legalizing drugs is a questionable strategy for reducing the profits to the cartels and the violence of the trade (Longmire 2011). There are two reasons that this counterargument only deserves to be addressed in passing. First, while it's difficult to accurately estimate the total profits of an illegal economy, it seems naive to suggest that the drug trade's enormous profits are not primarily made from drugs. No one ever claimed that legalizing drugs would eradicate crime in general. Second, this argument sidesteps the fact that prohibition does not serve a useful function, as discussed here and in countless other sources on the topic: it does not reduce the accessibility of drugs, it criminalizes the most vulnerable people involved (addicts), it imprisons the poorest in its ranks, and the richest and most powerful continue to turn a profit.

6. See Fernández-Vega 2012.

7. The question of whether there should be a distinction between illegal and legal economies and whether activities that are outlawed such as drug trafficking should be distinguished from earnings that

are unreported to the government is a heated one in the social sciences. As Venkatesh (2006) points out, the indeterminacy in how these distinctions are made is due to the arbitrary nature of how activities are categorized. This has resulted in a proliferation of terms that are often used synonymously for "informal economy," for example, *underground, illicit, black market, parallel,* and *alternative.*

REFERENCES

Abu-Lughod, Lila. 1987. *Veiled Sentiments: Honor and Poetry in a Bedouin Society.* Cairo: American University in Cairo Press.

———. 2008. *Writing Women's Worlds: Bedouin Stories.* Berkeley: University of California Press.

Adorno, Theodor W., and J. M. Bernstein. 1990. *The Culture Industry: Selected Essays on Mass Culture.* New York: Routledge.

Alexander, Michelle. 2010. *The New Jim Crow: Mass Incarceration in the Age of Colorblindness.* New York: New Press.

Altamirano, Magdalena. 2010. "Female Representations in the Mexican Traditional Ballad: Heroines and Antiheroines." *Revista de Dialectología y Tradiciones Populares* 65 (2): 445–64.

American Psychiatric Association. [1994] 2000. *Diagnostic and Statistical Manual of Mental Disorders: DSM-IV-TR.* Washington, DC: American Psychiatric Association.

Andreas, Peter. 1995. "Free Market Reform and Drug Market Prohibition: US Policies at Cross-Purposes in Latin America." *Third World Quarterly* 16 (1): 75–87.

———. 1996. "U.S.-Mexico: Open Markets, Closed Border." *Foreign Policy* 103: 51–69.

———. 1998. "The Political Economy of Narco-Corruption in Mexico." *Current History New York* 97 (618): 160–65.

———. 2009. *Border Games: Policing the U.S.-Mexico Divide.* Ithaca, NY: Cornell University Press.

Andreas, Peter, and Thomas J. Biersteker. 2003. *The Rebordering of North America: Integration and Exclusion in a New Security Context.* New York: Routledge.

Andreas, Peter, and Timothy Snyder. 2000. *The Wall around the West: State Borders and Immigration Controls in North America and Europe.* Lanham, MD: Rowman & Littlefield.

Anti-Fascist. 2012. "American Narcos: The Real 'Masters of Paradise.'" *Antifascist Calling . . . Exploring the Shadowlands of the Corporate Police State.* http://antifascist-calling.blogspot.ca/.

Associated Press. 2012. "9 Mexico Prison Guards Helped Gangsters Escape; 44 Members of Rival Gang Bludgeoned and Knifed to Death in Prison Riot." February 21.

Astorga Almanza, Luis Alejandro. 1997. "Los corridos de traficantes de drogas en México y Colombia." *Revista Mexicana de Sociología* 59 (4): 245–61.

———. 2001. "The Limits of Anti-Drug Policy in Mexico." *International Social Science Journal* 53 (169): 427–34.

———. 2003. *Drogas sin fronteras.* Miguel Hidalgo, Mexico: Grijalbo.

———. 2005. "Corridos de traficantes y censura." *Región y Sociedad* 17 (32): 145–65.

———. 2005. *El siglo de las drogas: El narcotrafico, del Porfiriato al nuevo milenio.* Mexico City: Plaza y Janés.

Bandow, Doug. 2012. "Will Mexico Declare Peace in the War on Drugs, and Will Obama Let Them?" *Forbes,* July 9.

Barclay, Eliza. 2004. "Bribing Guards a Way of Life in Mexico's Prisons; Low Pay for Guards Contributes to Corruption." *San Francisco Chronicle,* December 19.

Bartilow, H. A., and K. Eom. 2009. "Busting Drugs While Paying with Crime: The Collateral Damage of US Drug Enforcement in Foreign Countries." *Foreign Policy Analysis* 5 (2): 93–116.

Basch, Linda G., Nina Glick Schiller, and Cristina Szanton Blanc. 1994. *Nations Unbound: Transnational Projects, Postcolonial Predicaments, and Deterritorialized Nation-States.* New York: Gordon and Breach.

Beck, Ulrich, and Mark Ritter. 1992. *Risk Society: Towards a New Modernity*. New Delhi: Sage.

Beittel, June S. 2013. "Mexico's Drug Trafficking Organizations: Source and Scope of the Rising Violence." Congressional Research Service, April 15. www.fas.org/sgp/crs/row/R41576.pdf.

Bertram, Eva, Morris Blachman, Kenneth Sharpe and Peter Andrews. 1996. *Drug War Politics: The Price of Denial*. Berkeley: University of California Press.

Binder, Amy. 1993. "Constructing Racial Rhetoric: Media Depictions of Harm in Heavy Metal and Rap Music." *American Sociological Review* 58 (6): 753–67.

Blackstone, Samuel. 2012. "The Amount of Money Cartels Spend on Bribes Is Staggering." *Business Insider International*, June 15.

Blakely, Tony, Simon Hales, and Alistair Woodward. 2004. *Poverty: Assessing the Distribution of Health Risks by Socioeconomic Position at National and Local Levels*. Geneva: World Health Organization. Available at www.who.int/quantifying_ehimpacts/publications/ebd10.pdf.

Bourgois, Philippe. 2003. *In Search of Respect: Selling Crack in El Barrio*. Cambridge: Cambridge University Press.

Bourgois, Philippe I., and Jeff Schonberg. 2009. *Righteous Dopefiend*. Berkeley: University of California Press.

Bowden, Charles. 2002. *Down by the River: Drugs, Money, Murder, and Family*. New York: Simon & Schuster.

Bowden, Charles, and Javier Aguilar. 1998. *Juárez: The Laboratory of Our Future*. New York: Aperture.

Bowden, Charles, and Alice Leora Briggs. 2010. *Dreamland: The Way Out of Juárez*. Austin: University of Texas Press.

Bowden, Charles, and Julian Cardona. 2010. *Murder City: Ciudad Juárez and the Global Economy's New Killing Fields*. New York: Nation Books.

Burnett, John. 2010. "Drugs Cross Border by Truck, Free Trade, and Chance." National Public Radio (NPR), November 8.

Campbell, Howard. 2005. "Drug Trafficking Stories: Everyday Forms of Narco-Folklore on the US-Mexico Border." *International Journal of Drug Policy* 16 (5): 326–33.

————. 2008. "Female Drug Smugglers on the U.S.-Mexico Border: Gender, Crime, and Empowerment." *Anthropological Quarterly* 81 (1): 233–67.

————. 2009. *Drug War Zone: Frontline Dispatches from the Streets of El Paso and Juárez.* Austin: University of Texas Press.

————. 2012. "Narco-Propaganda in the Mexican 'Drug War': An Anthropological Perspective." *Latin American Perspectives.* Published online April 30, doi:10.1177/0094582X12443519.

Cardona, Julian. 2010. "Families Blame Mexico's Calderón over Massacre." Reuters, February 2. www.reuters.com/article/idUSTRE6115IJ20100203.

Carpenter, Ami C. 2010. "Beyond Drug Wars: Transforming Factional Conflict in Mexico." *Conflict Resolution Quarterly* 27 (4): 401–21.

Carrier, James. 1995. *Gifts and Commodities: Exchange and Western Capitalism since 1700.* New York: Routledge.

————. 2001. "Social Aspects of Abstraction." *Social Anthropology* 9 (3): 243–56.

Carrier, James G., and Daniel Miller. 1998. *Virtualism: A New Political Economy.* New York: Berg.

Castillo, E. Eduardo. 2010. "México limita depósitos de dólares para combatir lavado de dinero." *Excélsior,* June 18.

Cattelino, Jessica R. 2008. *High Stakes: Florida Seminole Gaming and Sovereignty.* Durham, NC: Duke University Press.

Cave, Damien. 2012. "In Mexico, a Kidnapping Ignored as Crime Worsens." *New York Times,* March 17.

Cevallos, Diego. 2008. "Church Uproar over Drug Traffickers' 'Good Works.'" Inter Press Service, April 8.

Clifford, James. 2001. "Indigenous Articulations." *Contemporary Pacific* 13 (2): 468–90.

Corchado, Alfredo. 2013. *Midnight in Mexico: A Reporter's Journey through a Country's Descent into Darkness.* New York: Penguin Books.

Cuddehe, Mary. 2011. "Myths and Realities about Drug Addiction in Mexico." *Lancet* 377 (9759): 15–16.

Das, Veena. 2003. "Trauma and Testimony: Implications for Political Community." *Anthropological Theory* 3 (3): 293–307.

————. 2007. *Life and Words: Violence and the Descent into the Ordinary.* Berkeley: University of California Press.

Davenport-Hines, R. P. T. 2001. *The Pursuit of Oblivion: A Global History of Narcotics, 1500–2000.* London: Weidenfeld & Nicolson.

Dávila, César Burgos. 2011. "Music and Drug Trafficking in Mexico: An Approach to Narcocorridos from the Notion of Mediator / Música y narcotráfico en México: Una aproximación a los narcocorridos desde la noción de mediador." *Athenea Digital* 11 (1).

de Barbieri, Teresita. 1993. "Sobre la categoría género: Una introducción teorico-metológica." *Debates en Sociología* 18: 2–19.

deBree, Jordan, and Clayton Worfolk, dirs. 2009. *Mexico: Dangerous Music.* Foreign Exchange with Daljit Dhaliwal. PBS, March 20.

Deleuze, Gilles. 1988. *Spinoza, Practical Philosophy.* San Francisco: City Lights Books.

Diaz-Cotto, Juanita. 2005. "Latinas and the War on Drugs in the United States, Latin America, and Europe." In *Global Lockdown: Race, Gender, and the Prison-Industrial Complex,* ed. J. Sudbury, 137–53. New York: Routledge.

Douglas, Mary. 1992. *Risk and Blame: Essays in Cultural Theory.* New York: Routledge.

Douglas, Mary, and Aaron B. Wildavsky. 1982. *Risk and Culture: An Essay on the Selection of Technological and Environmental Dangers.* Berkeley: University of California Press.

Duke, Steven B. 2009. "Drugs: To Legalize or Not." *Wall Street Journal,* April 25.

Dunn, Elizabeth. 2007. "Of Pufferfish and Ethnography: Plumbing New Depths in Economic Geography." In *Politics and Practice in Economic Geography,* ed. A. Tickell, 82–93. Los Angeles, CA: Sage.

Dwyer, Augusta. 1994. *On the Line: Life on the US-Mexican Border.* London: Latin America Bureau.

Economist. 2012. "Burn-Out and Battle Fatigue: As Violence Soars, So Do Voices of Dissent against Drug Prohibition." March 17.

Edberg, Cameron Mark. 2004a. *El Narcotraficante: Narcocorridos and the Construction of a Cultural Persona on the U.S.-Mexican Border.* Austin: University of Texas Press.

―――. 2004b. "The Narcotrafficker in Representation and Practice: A Cultural Persona from the U.S.-Mexican Border." *Ethos* 32 (2): 257–77.

Ellingwood, Ken. 2008. "Mexico Traffickers Bribed Former Anti-Drug Chief, Officials Say." *Los Angeles Times,* November 22.

―――. 2010. "Mexico Massacre Response Fails to Convince Officials' Suggestions That Youths Slain at Ciudad Juárez Teen Party Had Drug Ties, Anger Relatives." *Los Angeles Times,* February 4.

El Paso Intelligence Center (EPIC), Gang Intelligence Unit. 2011. "Language of the Cartels: Narco Terminology, Identifiers, and Clothing Style." Intelligence Information-Officer Safety Report, January 28. http://publicintelligence.net/ules-lulzsec-release-epic-language-of-the-cartels-narco-terminology-report/.

Ericson, Richard V., and Aaron Doyle, eds. 2003. *Risk and Morality.* Toronto: University of Toronto Press.

Fayerick, Deborah, Michael Cary, and Sheila Steffen. 2009. "Drug Smugglers Becoming More Creative, U.S. Agents Say." *CNN Online,* April 16. www.cnn.com/2009/CRIME/04/16/creative.drug.smugglers/.

Fernández-Vega, Carlos. 2012. "México SA." *La Jornada,* May 1.

Gaouette, Nicole. 2011. "Clinton Broaching Border Trucking, Drug Violence on Mexico Trip." Bloomberg, January 23. www.bloomberg.com/news/2011–01–21/clinton-to-visit-mexico-with-trucking-security-on-agenda.html.

Garcia, Angela. 2008. "The Elegiac Addict: History, Chronicity, and the Melancholic Subject." *Cultural Anthropology* 23 (4): 718–46.

―――. 2010. *Pastoral Clinic: Addiction and Dispossession along the Rio Grande.* Berkeley: University of California Press.

Gaviria, Alejandro, and Daniel Mejía, eds. 2011. *Anti-Drugs Policies in Colombia: Successes, Failures, and Wrong Turns.* Bogotá: Ediciones Uniandes.

Geertz, Clifford. 1973. *The Interpretation of Cultures: Selected Essays.* New York: Basic Books.

Gibler, John. 2011. *To Die in Mexico: Dispatches from Inside the Drug War.* San Francisco: City Lights.

Giddens, Anthony. 1990. *The Consequences of Modernity.* Stanford: Stanford University Press.

Gordillo, Gaston. 2004. *Landscapes of Devils: Tensions of Place and Memory in the Argentinean Chaco.* Durham, NC: Duke University Press.

Graeber, David. 2011. *Debt: The First 5,000 Years.* Brooklyn, NY: Melville House.

Gray, Herman. 1995. "Popular Music as a Social Problem: A Social History of Claims against Popular Music." In *Images of Issues: Typifying Contemporary Social Problems,* ed. J. Best, 143–58. New York: A. de Gruyter.

Grillo, Joan. 2009. "Drug-Dealing for Jesus: Mexico's Evangelical Narcos." *Time,* July 19.

Gutmann, Matthew C. 1993. "Rituals of Resistance." *Latin American Perspectives* 20 (2): 74–92.

———. 1997. "Trafficking in Men: The Anthropology of Masculinity." *Annual Review of Anthropology* 26 (1): 385.

Ho, Karen Zouwen. 2009. *Liquidated: An Ethnography of Wall Street.* Durham, NC: Duke University Press.

Human Rights Watch. 2008. "Mexico's National Human Rights Commission: A Critical Assessment." *Human Rights Watch* 20: 1(b). www.hrw.org/sites/default/files/reports/mexico0208_1.pdf.

———. 2011. "Neither Rights nor Security: Killings, Torture, and Disappearances in Mexico's 'War on Drugs.'" www.hrw.org/sites/default/files/reports/mexico1111webwcover_0.pdf.

Irwin, Robert McKee. 2003. *Mexican Masculinities.* Minneapolis: University of Minnesota Press.

Johnson, Phillip. 2011. "How to Identify a Narcotrafficker: Matador Network." http://matadornetwork.com/abroad/how-to-identify-a-narcotrafficker/.

Johnson, Tim. 2012. "Rehab Clinics Turn into Killing Zones in Mexico's Drug War." McClatchy Newspapers, May 14.

Keefe, Patrick Radden. 2012. "Cocaine Incorporated." *New York Times Magazine,* June 17, MM36.

Keesing, Roger. 1985. "Kwaio Women Speak: The Micropolitics of Autobiography in a Solomon Island Society." *American Anthropologist* 87 (1): 27–39.

Kimpel, Dan. 2009. "Jenni Rivera Is 'La Diva de la Banda.'" *Music World: Featuring BMI's Songwriters and Composers* 8 (3.12): July 13. www.bmi.com/musicworld/entry/jenni_rivera_is_la_diva_de_la_banda.

Klima, Alan. 2002. *The Funeral Casino: Meditation, Massacre, and Exchange with the Dead in Thailand*. Princeton, NJ: Princeton University Press.

Kocherga, Angela. 2011. "Churches in Mexico Accepting Donations from Drug Cartels." KVUE News, May 5. www.kvue.com/news/Churches-in-Mexico-accepting-donations-from-drug-cartels-121364079.html.

Kopinak, Kathryn. 1995. "Gender as a Vehicle for the Subordination of Women Maquiladora Workers in Mexico." *Latin American Perspectives* 22 (1): 30–48.

Kulick, Don. 2010. *Travesti: Sex, Gender, and Culture among Brazilian Transgendered Prostitutes*. Chicago: University of Chicago Press.

Li, Tania Murray. 2000. "Articulating Indigenous Identity in Indonesia: Resource Politics and the Tribal Slot." *Comparative Studies in Society and History* 42 (1): 149–79.

Limón, Graciela. 1994. *The Memories of Ana Calderón: A Novel*. Houston, TX: Arte Público Press.

Longmire, Sylvia. 2011. "Legalization Won't Kill the Cartels." *New York Times,* June 18.

Malkin, Elisabeth. 2010. "Death Toll in Juárez Attack Rises to 14." *New York Times,* October 28.

Malkin, Victoria. 2001. "Narcotrafficking, Migration, and Modernity in Rural Mexico." *Latin American Perspectives* 28 (4): 101–28.

Martinez, Edicio. 2010. "76-Year-Old Woman Busted with 3 Pounds of Cocaine." CBS News, October 22. www.cbsnews.com/8301-504083_162-20020452-504083.html.

Maurer, Bill. 2005. *Mutual Life, Limited: Islamic Banking, Alternative Currencies, Lateral Reason*. Princeton, NJ: Princeton University Press.

McDonald, James H. 2005. "The Narcoeconomy and Small-Town, Rural Mexico." *Human Organization* 64 (2): 115–25.

———. 2009. "The Cultural Effects of the Narcoeconomy in Rural Mexico." *Journal of International and Global Studies* 1 (1): 1–29.

McDonald, James R. 1988. "Censoring Rock Lyrics: A Historical Analysis of the Debate." *Youth & Society* 19 (3): 294–313.

McDowell, John H. 2000. *Poetry and Violence: The Ballad Tradition of Mexico's Costa Chica*. Urbana: University of Illinois Press.

McLuhan, Marshall. 1994. *Understanding Media: The Extensions of Man*. Cambridge, MA: MIT Press.

Miller, Bruce G. 2003. *Invisible Indigenes: The Politics of Nonrecognition.* Lincoln: University of Nebraska Press.

Miskimmin, Susanne. 2008. "When Aboriginal Equals 'at Risk': The Impact of an Institutional Keyword on Aboriginal Head Start Families." In *Words, Worlds, and Material Girls: Language, Gender, Globalization,* ed. B. S. McElhinny, 107–28. Berlin: Mouton de Gruyter.

Mondaca Cota, Anajilda. 2004. *Las mujeres también pueden: Género y narcocorrido.* Sinaloa, Mexico: Universidad de Occidente.

Muehlmann, Shaylih. 2008. "'Spread Your Ass Cheeks': And Other Things That Should Not Be Said in Indigenous Languages." *American Ethnologist* 35 (1): 34–48.

———. 2009. "How Do Real Indians Fish? Neoliberal Multiculturalism and Contested Indigeneities at the End of the Colorado River." *American Anthropologist* 111 (4): 468–79.

———. 2013. *Where the River Ends: Contested Indigeneity in the Mexican Colorado Delta.* Durham, NC: Duke University Press.

National Commission on Law Observance and Enforcement. 1931. "Report on the Enforcement of the Prohibition Laws of the United States." January 7. www.ncjrs.gov/pdffiles1/Digitization/44540NCJRS.pdf.

National Drug Enforcement Intelligence Center. 2011. "National Drug Threat Assesssment." August. www.justice.gov/archive/ndic/pubs44/44849/44849p.pdf.

National Public Radio. 2007. "Timeline: America's War on Drugs." April 2. www.npr.org/templates/story/story.php?storyId=9252490.

New York Times. 2012. "Too Big to Indict." Editorial, December 11. www.nytimes.com/2012/12/12/opinion/hsbc-too-big-to-indict.html?_r=0.

Niezen, Ronald. 2003. *The Origins of Indigenism: Human Rights and the Politics of Identity.* Berkeley: University of California Press.

Nordstrom, Carolyn. 2007. *Global Outlaws: Crime, Money, and Power in the Contemporary World.* Berkeley: University of California Press.

Ochoa, Ana María. 2006. "A Manera de Introducción: La materialidad de lo musical y su relación con la violencia." *TRANS Revista Transcultural de Música* 10. www.sibetrans.com/trans/a142/a-manera-deintroduccion-la-materialidad-de-lo-musical-y-su-relacion-con-la-violencia.

Ovemex. 2011a. "Mexican Smugglers Have New Ruse; Hiding Drugs in the Vehicles of Unsuspecting Border Commuters." *Borderland Beat: Reporting on the Mexican Cartel Drug War,* July 7. www.borderlandbeat. com/2011/07/mexican-smugglers-have-new-ruse-hiding.html.

———. 2011b. "Narco-Corrido Singer Gerardo Ortiz Attacked in Colima." *Borderland Beat: Reporting on the Mexican Cartel Drug War,* March 20. www.borderlandbeat.com/2011/03/narco-corrido-singer-gerardo-ortiz.html.

Papenfus, Mary. 2011. "It Was 'Kill or Be Killed,' Says Boy Who Worked for Mexican Drug Cartel." *The Newser.* www.newser.com /tag/26460/2/teenager.html.

Paredes, Américo. 2003. "The United States, Mexico, and Machismo." In *Perpectives on Las Américas: A Reader in Culture, History and Representation,* ed. M.C. Gutmann, F.V. Matos Rodríguez, L. Stephen, and P. Zavella, 329–41. Oxford: Blackwell.

Paredes, Américo, and Richard Bauman. 1993. *Folklore and Culture on the Texas-Mexican Border.* Austin: CMAS Books, Center for Mexican American Studies, University of Texas at Austin.

Perez, Pablo. 2012. "Women on the Rise in Mexican Drug Cartels." Associated Press, May 27.

Perramond, Eric. 2004. "Desert Traffic: The Dynamics of the Drug Trade in Northwestern Mexico." In *Dangerous Harvest,* ed. M. Steinberg, J. Hobbs, and K. Mathewson, 209–17. Oxford: Oxford University Press.

Pew Research Center. 2012. "Mexicans Back Military Campaign against Cartels Despite Doubts about Success, Human Rights Costs." Global Attitudes Project, June 20. www.pewglobal.org /files/2012/06/Pew-Global-Attitudes-Project-Mexico-Report-FINAL-Wednesday-June-20-2012.pdf.

Quinones, Sam. 2001. *True Tales from Another Mexico: The Lynch Mob, the Popsicle Kings, Chalino, and the Bronx.* Albuquerque: University of New Mexico Press.

Ramírez, Arturo. 1990. "Views of the Corrido Hero: Paradigm and Development." *Americas Review* 18 (2): 71–79.

Rawlins, Amy. 2011. "Mexico's Drug War." Council on Foreign Relations, December 13. www.cfr.org/mexico/mexicos-drug-war/p13689.

Reyes, Francisco. 2012. "Dancing to the Beat of Hypocrisy." *El Paisano,* February 21.

Rosenbaum, Jill Leslie, and Lorraine Prinsky. 1991. "The Presumption of Influence: Recent Responses to Popular Music Subcultures." *Crime & Delinquency* 37 (4): 528–35.

Rosenberg, Mica. 2010. "Corrupt, Insecure Prisons Undermine Mexico Drug War." Reuters, August 18.

———. 2012. "Attack on Mexican Drug Rehab Center Leaves 11 Dead." Reuters, June 4.

Rydell, C. Peter, and Susan S. Everingham. Rand Corp. Santa Monica. 1994. "Controlling Cocaine: Supply versus Demand Programs." www.dtic.mil/cgibin/GetTRDoc?AD=ADA282676&Location=U2 &doc=GetTRDoc.pdf.

Santamaría, Arturo. 2012. *Las jefas del narco: El ascenso de las mujeres en el crimen organizado.* Mexico City: Grijalbo Mondadori.

Sarmiento, Tomas, and Miguel Gutierrez. 2011. "Mexico Passes Law to Combat Cartel Money Laundering." Reuters, October 11.

Saviano, Roberto. 2012. "Where the Mob Keeps Its Money." *New York Times,* August 25.

Schiller, Nina Glick, Linda G. Basch, and Cristina Szanton Blanc. 1992. *Towards a Transnational Perspective on Migration: Race, Class, Ethnicity, and Nationalism Reconsidered.* New York: New York Academy of Sciences.

Simonett, Helena. 2006. "'Los Gallos Valientes': Examining Violence in Mexican Popular Music." *TRANS-Transcultural Music Review* 10. www.sibetrans.com/trans/a149/los-gallos-valientes-examining-violence-in-mexican-popular-music.

Singer, Merrill. 2006. *The Face of Social Suffering: The Life History of a Street Drug Addict.* Long Grove, IL: Waveland Press.

———. 2008. *Drugging the Poor: Legal and Illegal Drugs and Social Inequality.* Long Grove, IL: Waveland Press.

Syal, Rajeev. 2009. "Drug Money Saved Banks in Global Crisis, Claims UN Advisor." *Guardian,* Sunday, December 13.

Taibbi, Matt. 2012. "Outrageous HSBC Settlement Proves the Drug War Is a Joke." *Rolling Stone,* December 20.

Tsing, Anna Lowenhaupt. 2005. *Friction: An Ethnography of Global Connection*. Princeton, NJ: Princeton University Press.

Tuckman, Jo. 2012. "Mexico Journalists Tortured and Killed by Drug Cartels." *Guardian*, May 4.

UN Office on Drugs and Crime (UNODC). 2010. *World Drug Report*. New York: United Nations Publication. www.unodc.org/documents/wdr /WDR_2010/World_Drug_Report_2010_lo-res.pdf.

———. 2011. *Estimating Illicit Financial Flows Resulting from Drug Trafficking and Other Transnational Organized Crimes*. Vienna: United Nations Publication. www.unodc.org/documents/data-and-analysis/Studies/Illicit_financial_flows_2011_web.pdf.

———. 2012. *World Drug Report 2012*. Vienna: United Nations Publication. www.unodc.org/documents/data-and-analysis/WDR2012/WDR_ 2012_web_small.pdf.

U.S. Department of Justice, National Drug Intelligence Center (NDIC). 2011. "National Drug Threat Assessment 2011." www.justice.gov /archive/ndic/pubs44/44849/44849p.pdf.

U.S. Government Accountability Office. 2007. *DRUG CONTROL: U.S. Assistance Has Helped Mexican Counternarcotics Efforts, but Tons of Illicit Drugs Continue to Flow into the United States*. Report to Congress. GAO-07–1018. www.gao.gov/new.items/d071018.pdf.

Valdés, Teresa, and José Olavarría. 1998. *Masculinidades y equidad de género en América Latina*. Santiago, Chile: FLASCO.

Valdez-Cárdenas, Javier. 2011. "Restaurantes y bares de Sinaloa no podrán difundir narcocorridos." *La Jornada*, May 19.

Valenzuela Arce, Jose Manuel. 2002. *Jefe de jefes: Corridos y narcocultura en México*. Mexico City: Plaza y Janés.

Venkatesh, Sudhir Alladi. 2006. *Off the Books: The Underground Economy of the Urban Poor*. Cambridge, MA: Harvard University Press.

Villalobos, Jose Pablo, and Juan Carlos Ramírez-Pimienta. 2004. "Corridos and La Pura Verdad: Myths and Realities of the Mexican Ballad." *South Central Review* 21 (3): 129–49.

Viveros, Mara. 1997. "Los estudios sobre lo masculino en América Latina: Una producción teórica emergente." *Nomadas* 6 (March). www.ucentral.edu.co/images/stories/iesco/revista_nomadas/6/nomadas_6_4_ los_estudios_masculino.pdf.

Viveros, Mara, Norma Fuller, and José Olavarria. 2001. "Hombres e identidades de género: Investigaciones desde América Latina." *CEDA-IDEA* 1 (July): 370.

Vulliamy, Ed. 2012. "Western Banks 'Reaping Billions from Colombian Cocaine Trade.'" *Guardian,* June 2.

Wald, Elijah. 2002. "Narcocorridos: A New Ballad Tradition." *Sing Out! The Folk Song Magazine* 46 (1): 72–73.

Weiner, Annette B. 1976. *Women of Value, Men of Renown: New Perspectives in Trobriand Exchange.* Austin: University of Texas Press.

Wilkinson, Tracy. 2009. "Women Play a Bigger Role in Mexico's Drug War." *Los Angeles Times,* November 10.

———. 2012. "Parts of at Least 15 Bodies Found Near Lake Chapala." *Los Angeles Times,* Foreign Desk, May 10.

Wright, Melissa. 2011. "Necropolitics, Narcopolitics, and Femicide: Gendered Violence on the Mexico-U.S. Border." *Signs* 36 (3): 707.

INDEX

Page numbers in italics *indicate illustrations.*